The

THREADS

OF READING

STRATEGIES FOR
LITERACY DEVELOPMENT

 KAREN TANKERSLEY

ASCD

Association for Supervision and Curriculum Development
Alexandria, Virginia USA

Association for Supervision and Curriculum Development
1703 N. Beauregard St. • Alexandria, VA 22311-1714 USA
Telephone: 800-933-2723 or 703-578-9600 • Fax: 703-575-5400
Web site: http://www.ascd.org • E-mail: member@ascd.org

Gene R. Carter, *Executive Director;* Nancy Modrak, *Director of Publishing;* Julie Houtz, *Director of Book Editing & Production;* Deborah Siegel, *Project Manager;* Reece Quiñones, *Senior Graphic Designer;* Jim Beals, *Typesetter;* Dina Seamon, *Production Coordinator.*

ASCD publications present a variety of viewpoints. The views expressed or implied in this book should not be interpreted as official positions of the Association.

Printed in the United States of America.

November 2003 member book for non-U.S. members only (pc). ASCD Premium, Comprehensive, and Regular members periodically receive ASCD books as part of their membership benefits. No. FY04-2a.

Paperback ISBN: 0-87120-794-X * ASCD product #103316 * List Price: $25.95
  ($20.95 ASCD member price, direct from ASCD only)
e-books ($25.95): netLibrary ISBN 0-87120-952-7 * ebrary 0-87120-941-1

Library of Congress Cataloging-in-Publication Data

Tankersley, Karen, 1952-
  Threads of reading : strategies for literacy development / Karen Tankersley.
      p. cm.
Includes bibliographical references and index.
  ISBN 0-87120-794-X (alk. paper)
  1. Reading. 2. Literacy. I. Title.
  LB1050.T27 2003
  371.41--dc22

                                        2003018217

12 11 10 09 08 07 06 05 04 03   12 11 10 9 8 7 6 5 4 3 2 1

The

THREADS

OF READING

STRATEGIES FOR
LITERACY DEVELOPMENT

⅜ Preface ⅝

In December of 2000, the National Reading Panel, a group convened to study the scientific research in the field of literacy, released a report summarizing their findings. This group identified five key areas of reading instruction: Phonemic Awareness, Phonics Instruction, Fluency, Comprehension, and Vocabulary Instruction. As a reading specialist and administrator, I was pleased to see the five areas summarized and presented by the panel, but to me there was a missing piece of the puzzle. I felt that there was a sixth thread that was also an important part of the teaching of reading. This thread was all the "higher-order skills" that go beyond basic comprehension and allow students to evaluate, analyze, interpret, and synthesize. It is this thread that most upper-grade teachers struggle to help students develop in middle school and high school and even into the college years. As our world continues to evolve into a more science-based, technological, and global society, it is this thread that will be required for the workforce of tomorrow. Because it is so vital that students be able to think and process at the levels of analysis, synthesis, evaluation, and interpretation, this thread must not be lost in the broader context of simple "comprehension." Just as phonemic awareness is a precursor to solid decoding, basic comprehension skills are a precursor to the higher-order thinking thread. It is clear to me from watching students develop as readers over the years that each of these factors is vital to the tapestry of reading and that no aspect of the reading tapestry can be missing if children are to become successful, thinking, and literate adults.

❧ Acknowledgments ❧

This book is dedicated to two women who made a difference in my own literacy development. The first is my mother, who exposed me to wonderful stories, rhymes, riddles, poems, and information that immersed me in print as soon as I was old enough to sit on her lap and listen. Books were constant companions in our home as I was growing up. Every trip to the grocery brought two new "golden books" to fill my bedroom bookshelf and stimulate my interest in becoming a lifelong reader and learner.

The second woman is Mrs. Gardiner, my senior AP English teacher. Mrs. Gardiner was the model of what a good literacy teacher should be. An avid reader herself, she modeled enthusiasm for literature in all forms. She demanded excellence from me in my literary analysis, interpretations, and critiques. She required that I stretch my capabilities in writing and would not settle for less than my best. My hope is that other students along the way will also meet a "Mrs. Gardiner" who will stimulate, challenge, and bring out the best in them as well.

⚜ Introduction ⚜

The art of teaching reading is like weaving a beautiful tapestry.
Like every tapestry, reading knowledge is made up of tightly woven,
strong foundational threads. Each thread must be present
to make the tapestry strong, able to withstand lifelong use,
and functional through all seasons.

Effective readers know how to apply decoding skills to recognize words quickly and efficiently. Effective readers have good vocabularies in relation to their age and show high word recognition. Effective readers possess strong fluency skills. They can read with good expression, intonation, pitch, and phrasing. Effective readers understand and remember what they read. They can summarize and discuss material, and demonstrate comprehension of the text. Finally, effective readers can analyze and evaluate what is being read, synthesize the material, and make interpretations regarding the content of the material.

Effective readers have solid phonemic awareness and understand how to use phonics skills to decode words they encounter while reading. They have automaticity in word identification. Effective readers read with fluency and good expression. They have good comprehension. Effective readers can use world knowledge and background information to draw valid inferences and conclusions from texts, use comprehension monitoring strategies and repair strategies while reading, and use their knowledge of spelling patterns to assist with possible pronunciations of words they encounter while reading to increase comprehension.

Effective readers are able to think about and evaluate what they are reading while they are processing and decoding the text.

Reading is a complex process made up of several interlocking skills and processes. The sum of these pieces is a tapestry that good readers use on a day-to-day basis to process text in their world. The tapestry of effective reading is woven from six foundational threads. Without each thread being present in the tapestry of an individual's reading abilities, there are holes and the weave cannot hold tight and cannot function for lifelong use. This book is for educators at all levels charged with helping to form the tapestry of literacy in their students. It presents the research behind each thread as well as many ideas for how skillful literacy and content-area teachers can structure the classroom environment to strengthen each thread. While some threads are more foundational than others, each thread is equally important and must be strongly woven into the tapestry. No strand can be missing. The six essential threads of reading are

1. Readiness/Phonemic Awareness.
2. Phonics and Decoding.
3. Fluency.
4. Vocabulary and Word Recognition.
5. Comprehension.
6. Higher-Order Thinking.

Reading does not have "traits" or "components" that can stand alone and be taught as isolated skills to students. The act of reading is an interlocking whole—a weave of many skills and understandings. We must, therefore, weave foundational threads that grow ever tighter and stronger as the tapestry pattern begins to emerge in our students. Only when the foundation is strong can we begin to add the "decorative" pattern of higher-level processing to the emerging tapestry. When children do not have solid threads woven into their reading development, holes in the reading process develop and the whole fabric weakens. We see the results of this weakness in our middle and high school classrooms every day. Students come to us without adequate background skills, so the act of reading is difficult and troublesome for them. We can no longer allow this to happen. The world of tomorrow requires not only skillful readers but also high-level thinkers and processors of knowledge. As educators, we can no longer leave reading development for some but not for others. We must become master weavers for our students so that each individual can prosper in the competitive world of tomorrow.

While weaving is a complex process, it is an easily learned skill when learned from good mentors. Educators at all levels must be those mentors. There are many ways that good teachers can weave each thread in the classroom on a daily basis. The most effective teachers continue to demonstrate that effective literacy instruction is a balance of explicit teaching as well as holistic reading and writing experiences that, when combined, produce more capable readers (Pressley et al., 1998). Over the years, I began collecting some of these "weaving strategies" so that others might also learn to weave reading magic in their own classrooms. This collection is a compendium of "teacher lore" that has been gathered from actual classroom practice. Whenever possible, I tried to cite the original source of the idea or technique. In most cases, I found the same ideas in perhaps slightly different forms in multiple sources across multiple years, so tracing the original owner of an idea or technique was an almost impossible task. I hope that this framework and the ideas gathered here will help each teacher clarify in his or her own mind how the tapestry of reading is woven for each individual learner. Good teachers know that a wide variety of methods and strategies help build strong learners and that students respond differently according to their own backgrounds and learning styles. This volume contains reading ideas, strategies, and techniques that teachers can use to add variety to their teaching to strengthen the weave in the literacy tapestry. While some strategies are clearly more effective at the primary level and some more effective at the upper grade level, most of the strategies can be adapted with a little teacher creativity to work with all age levels. Teachers in content-area classrooms will also find strategies and techniques that they can modify to suit the age and subject matter they teach. As you use these strategies and invent new techniques or modifications of some of the ideas in this volume, I hope that you will send me additional ideas and share the techniques or strategies that are working to help build student literacy and high reading achievement in your own classroom. You can reach me by e-mail at www.threadsofreading.com.

✷1✷

Readiness/Phonemic Awareness

Teaching children to manipulate the sounds in language helps all types of readers learn to read. Phonemic awareness and letter knowledge have been identified in several research studies (Anderson, Hiebert, Scott, & Wilkerson, 1985; Adams, 1990; Snow, Burns, & Griffin, 1998) as the two key indicators of how well children will master beginning reading skills during the first two years in school. Because it plays such a vital role in forming the foundation of reading development, phonemic awareness is the first thread in the tapestry of reading. Phonemic awareness is the ability to hear and manipulate phonemes, which are the smallest part of a spoken language. Phonemes are the element of language that allows discrimination and make a difference in the meaning of a specific word. In the English language, it is generally accepted that there are anywhere from 41 to 51 phonemes in spoken speech. While there are words with only one phoneme such as *I* or *a*, most words have more than one phoneme. More than one letter (such as in the phonemes "bl" or "ch") can also represent phonemes. Phonemes with more than one letter are usually referred to as blends, diphthongs, or digraphs depending on their composition.

Instruction in phonemic awareness involves helping children examine and manipulate phonemes in spoken syllables and words. The ability to recognize that words are made up of discrete sounds and that these sounds can be changed is essential to success in learning to read (Lundberg, Frost, & Petersen, 1988; Hoffman, Cunningham, Cunningham, & Yopp, 1998). Beginning readers must also be able to make the connection that words are made up of sounds and that sounds are made up of letters and letter combinations (Gunning, 1996). This understanding is the foundation on which to build solid reading skills.

One of the major components that determines a child's readiness to learn to read is his or her understanding of how the sounds work together. Children learn that words are made up of individual phonemes that help to make one word distinguishable from another word. For example, the words *cat, sat,* and *rat* have the same phoneme sound "at" at the end of the word but because of the initial phoneme difference, a listener interprets very different meanings for each word. Phonemic awareness is this ability to take words apart, to put them back together again, and to change them to something else. It is a foundational skill around which the rest of the threads of reading are woven.

In addition to understanding sounds, a child also needs to understand the concept of a word, how the position of a word (first word or last word) makes a difference in a sentence, and that words consist of individual letters. Children must also understand that letters have positions in words (first letter, middle letters, or last letter) and that some of these letters form syllables.

Some ways to help students develop their phonemic awareness abilities are through various activities that identify phonemes and syllables, sort and classify phonemes, blend phonemes to make words, break apart words into their various components, and interchange phonemes to make new words.

Why Is Phonemic Awareness Important?

According to the National Reading Panel Report (National Institute of Child Health and Human Development, 2000), the level of phonemic awareness that children possess when first beginning reading instruction and their knowledge of letters are the two best predictors of how well they will learn to read during the first two years of formal reading instruction. Researchers Adams, Foorman, Lundberg, & Beeler (1998) tell us that before children learn to read, they must understand that the sounds that are paired with the letters are the same as the sounds of speech they hear. They state, "For those of us who already know how to read and write, this realization seems very basic, almost transparent. Nevertheless, research shows that the very notion that spoken language is made up of sequences of these little sounds does not come naturally or easily to human beings" (p. 1). A strong understanding of phonemic concepts must be solidly in place prior to formal instruction in reading. It is critical that a child make the association that words on the page are simply "talk written down."

Children form concepts about literacy by observing adults in their environment and by interacting with print during their own early attempts at reading and writing (Sulzby & Teale, 1991). The first signs of phonemic awareness usually appear in children between the age of two and three years old when they begin making rhymes out of words that they know. For example, children may sing, recite rhymes, or make a game out of saying words like "sat, fat, cat, rat, bat, at." An extensive exposure to alliterative texts and rich oral environments during these early years helps ensure that this connection develops.

Young children start out believing that the "story" in a book is in the pictures. As they mature, they develop the understanding that while they cannot read the words, it is the words and not the pictures that carry the important meaning of the book (Snow, Burns, & Griffin, 1998). This is an important developmental milestone. Four- and five-year-old children can be observed to "read" books that adults have frequently read to them with increasing intonation and phrasing even though they are in reality only "pretend reading" a memorized book. Children frequently use certain patterns that they have learned from listening to children's books such as "once upon a time" or "the end" while pretend-reading their own books. In their early stages of writing development, these are also the styles that children will mimic in their own attempts at story writing.

Young children also develop some understanding of letters as they "write" on paper. At the age of two or three, many children have observed adults writing—so they make their own attempts at writing by making squiggles on paper. Often children can even "read" the message to anyone who asks for a "translation." In later stages of development, the squiggles the child makes may even become recognizable letters or letter strings. This development should be encouraged and supported in the preschool classroom and in the family. It is foundational development in the understanding of the link between writing and word messages.

Because they often hear stories being read aloud, young children may believe that "reading" only occurs when words are being spoken. When watching an adult read silently, the child may insist that something must be spoken for reading to be taking place (Ferreiro & Teberosky, 1982). Five year olds who have observed adults read silently will often engage in intense scrutiny of the pictures page by page as if reading silently before "reading" the page to another person. As children make more intense connections between the print and the "message" of the book, they will begin to attend more to the print on the page and less and less to the pictures. This transition seems to mark a period of time when children are assimilating knowledge about how print and speech are linked. This too is a developmental milestone on the road to fluent reading.

As children listen to adults read, they begin to develop the understanding that the adults are interpreting the message on the page through symbols. At quite a young age, children grasp the notion that an object or symbol can stand for a concept (Marzolf & De Loache, 1994). For example, children recognize that the "golden arches" stands for McDonald's restaurants long before they can read the name on the building. The interpretation of the child's own written symbols indicates that the child has made a connection between "talk" and the letter symbols on the page. This signals an emergence of sound-symbol awareness in the young child's mind.

Many children come from print-rich, literate homes and can have more than a thousand hours of exposure to reading and literacy-building activities before they enter formal school. In these homes, reading is a priority and parents have spent many hours reading to their children or playing language-building games such as singing, reciting rhymes, or playing word and letter games. Electronic letter identification technology, letter flash cards, and word games also abound in these homes. Writing is also encouraged and children have many opportunities to try a hand at scribbling, coloring, or working with magnetic letters. These children often "pretend read" a memorized book to their proud parents and "write" a love note to mommy or grandma. Their phonemic awareness skills are firmly in place by the time they enter formal schooling and they are ready to move into more formal reading activities.

What Happens When Phonemic Awareness Is Missing or Underdeveloped?

While phonemic awareness is easily taught to children in the early years, the absence of strong oral language, reading, and word play in the home can lead to reading difficulties and a failure to progress in reading development (Hammill & McNutt, 1980; Scarborough, 1998). The level of phonemic awareness that a child possesses accounts for as much as 50 percent of the variance in reading proficiency by the end of 1st grade (Blachman, 1991; Juel, 1991; Stanovich, 1986; Wagner, Torgeson, & Roshotte, 1994). The degree of phonemic awareness that the child has developed upon entry into school is widely held to be the strongest single determinant of the child's reading success (Adams, 1990; Stanovich, 1986; Snow, Burns, & Griffin, 1998).

Poorly developed phonemic awareness skills distinguish low socioeconomic preschoolers from their more advantaged peers (Liberman, Rubin, Duques, & Carlisle, 1985). According to researchers Snow, Burns, & Griffin (1998), "Cognitive studies of reading have identified phonological processing as crucial to successful reading and so it seems logical to suspect that poor readers may have phonological processing problems." Between 40 and 75 percent of preschoolers with early language impairments develop reading difficulties and other academic problems as they enter formal schooling (Aram & Hall, 1989; Brashir & Scavuzzo, 1992). Other factors besides an impoverished oral environment in the preschool years, such as attention deficit disorder or hyperactivity disorders, can also impair early success in reading development.

As many as 31 percent of the children who enter kindergarten with attention deficit or hyperactivity disorders will have difficulty learning to read. Initial problems in reading usually do not go away without intensive intervention and individualized tutoring. By 9th grade, over 50 percent of students with attention deficit or hyperactivity disorders will have developed moderate to severe reading delays or other reading problems (Shaywitz, Fletcher, & Shaywitz, 1994; 1995). Early monitoring and early support for these students is critical if they are to progress with their age peers.

One sometimes overlooked problem that makes it difficult for some children to learn distinguishing characteristics of words is the dialect of adult speakers who instruct them. Adult speakers often enunciate sounds differently based on their dialectic patterns and personal speech habits. This can make it difficult for a struggling child to clearly hear the word that the adult is trying to say. When an adult uses a different dialect than the child, special care must be taken to enunciate the phonemes clearly and distinctly.

Another reason that some children can be delayed in phonemic awareness skills is due to poor or slowly developing oral language skills. Sometimes children are not able to enunciate all of the phonemes they may be exposed to in oral language. Children who have had many ear infections or tubes in their ears as an infant, sometimes cannot discriminate all of the phoneme sounds in the English language. In addition to not being able to hear these sounds, children sometimes are not able to orally form some of them. Speech articulation is tied to developmental stages so children are not able to form all sounds by the same age. If there are concerns about a student's ability to discriminate or enunciate certain sounds, a speech pathologist should be consulted. In most cases, all sounds should be fully developed and present in a child's speech pattern by the age of eight or nine at the very latest. Failure to note these difficulties and seek advice could contribute to delays in the development of solid phonemic awareness skills in young readers.

Letter-Sound Identification

Once a child has a strong sense of phonemics, the learning of the letter names and their corresponding sounds can begin to take root. Learning letter sounds by associating the sound with something concrete such as an animal name or other concrete object is the quickest and most long-lasting method for learning the letters and their corresponding sounds. Teaching the letter names and letter sounds themselves is the beginning stage of phonics instruction.

The development of solid phonemic awareness skills should be the main goal of the preschool and kindergarten years. Early instruction in phonemic awareness should be primarily oral with the exception of some beginning attempts to write the letters themselves. There is a hierarchy of understandings that must be mastered at the foundational level (Treiman & Zukowski, 1991). The first understanding is the concept of a "word" followed by the concept of rhyme and how to make rhymes. After mastering these concepts, students must learn to segment syllables, hear the onset and rime in a word, and then learn to segment and blend sounds into words. Each child must be able to identify individual sounds within a word, recognize the same sounds in different words, and be able to distinguish between the same or different sounds in words. Children must also be able to combine sounds to form various words and to isolate separate sounds in words. Manipulating letters, sounds, and phonemes is the heart of learning to read.

An easy test to determine a child's readiness for beginning reading instruction is the letter identification test. Asking students to name letters and sounds given in random order is as good a predictor of reading readiness as is giving an entire reading readiness battery to the student (Snow, Burns, & Griffin, 1998). Developing phonological awareness consists of helping students understand the rhythm, pattern, and beauty of the language. Solid readiness skills consist of several factors. First, children must understand the concept of directionality. This understanding includes the concepts of left to right; front to back; and top to bottom. Second, they must learn to see and recognize patterns and develop an interest in the rhythm of language. According to Adams (1990), "Reading depends on a system of skills whose components must mesh properly." Understanding how print works and that it has predictable patterns help children learn to embrace print as enjoyable and helpful.

Children come to formal schooling with a wide range of background experiences and developmental milestones. Children should be taken from where they are and advanced in their reading development process. If kindergarten children already possess sound phonemic awareness skills when they come to school, then they are ready for more challenging work and more formal reading instruction. If they do not have this background, then we must provide this background knowledge and support before continuing with more advanced reading instruction.

Students who are extremely delayed or who come from severely impoverished homes may need additional tutoring or individual support to become proficient in letter-sound relationships. If children are having difficulty learning the letter names, we should teach the letters in unlike pairs such as *x* and *o* or *n* and *p*. Once the children have mastered the unlike letters, then they can advance to finer discriminations such as *c* and *o*, *r* and *n*, *m* and *n*, *b* and *d*, or *p* and *q*.

The phonemic awareness and extensiveness of the vocabulary that a kindergartner brings to school are two of the strongest predictors of future reading achievement (Juel, 1991; Scarborough, 1989; Stanovich, 1986; Wagner, Torgeson, & Roshotte, 1994). There is also a high correlation between letter identification skills and success in beginning reading (Scanlon & Vellutino, 1996). One of the main goals of the preschool and kindergarten years should be to have every child develop strong phonemic awareness skills and to master letter-sound identification. Beginning instruction in phonics prior to when the child has acquired phonemic awareness and letter identification skills is ineffective. Ensuring that these two foundational understandings were in place by the end of the kindergarten year would go a long way toward helping 1st graders develop solid beginning reading skills. Some activities to help students develop letter identification and letter-sound identification skills, are the following:

Letter Sort

Give students magnetic letters, lettercards, or letter tiles. Ask students to sort the letters by various categories such as letters with curves, letters with circles, long letters, tall letters, short letters, upper case, lower case, vowels, consonants, letters with short sticks, letters with long sticks, and so forth. This activity will help students visually identify the characteristics of the various letters and will reinforce the concept of sorting based on specific attributes.

Forming Letters

Ask students to form letters using various manipulative materials. Substances that can be used are clay, dough, sand, salt, or shaving cream. Grocery store meat trays work well as individual "drawing boards" for letter experimentation. Many grocery stores will give unused styrofoam meat packing trays to teachers free of charge or at a very minimal cost if you ask the store manager. Place alphabet stamps with blank paper in another center for student experimentation with letters. Cookie cutters to make letters from clay or play dough can also be available for making words in another classroom center.

Ordering Letters

Use a pointer often to help young children learn left-to-right tracking and sweep. Sing the alphabet song while pointing to the letters with the pointer. When lining up to leave the classroom, hand each child an alphabet letter. Sing the alphabet song with children and invite children to line up when the class sings their letter. After the children have lined up, double check that they are in ABC order by again singing the song and pointing to each child. If students are not in the correct place, ask them to determine what is wrong and how to fix it. Give them the opportunity to think through the process and to repair the problem.

Class Murals and Books

Create a class alphabet mural with each letter illustrated with a picture of an object that goes with each letter. Create class versions of alphabet books around themes such as holidays, animals, or circus items. Laminate the books and place them in centers for students to read and examine often.

Name Displays

Take a picture of each child in the class. Place the names of each student on a large word card and display the pictures and the name cards in alphabetical order on a bulletin board. Place letters that do not have student names associated with them on cards and place these in the proper order as "placeholders" in the alphabetic sequence. Spend time going over the various initial and interior sounds of the student names with the class until students have a good understanding of the components of each name. When students can't remember how to write or pronounce a particular letter, have them refer to the wall chart. For example, you could say, "That letter is written like the "b" in Bobby's name. Can you find his name on our wall alphabet chart?"

Word Transformations

Older struggling students can also work with manipulative words to get a better sense of letter relationships and patterns. Using a set of individual letters (magnetic, paper, or letter tiles), have small groups of students experiment with the letters to make lists of words that can be made into other words by either adding or subtracting one letter. Some examples would be *trip* to *rip*; *blend* to *lend*; and *light* to *flight*. See which group of students can find the longest list of words. A more advanced game would be to add two letters to the root word to create a different word. Letters can be added as either initial sounds, final sounds, or as a combination of both initial and final sounds.

Teaching Students to Recognize Syllables

Once students understand what words are, they are then ready to move to understanding that words are made up of syllables. When students understand that words contain one or more syllables, they can then master the concept of rhyme. Helping students examine small parts of words as individual syllables will help students make the link between being able to hear and manipulate phonemes. This skill forms the backbone of phonemic awareness in children. Some strategies to teach the syllable concept are:

Word Comparisons

To increase student awareness of the number of syllables in a word and how this affects the number of letters it will contain, show students two words of various lengths that they cannot yet read. Pronounce the two words and ask students to predict which word belongs to which spoken word. For example, show the written words "pen" and "pencil" to students, asking students to identify which word they think would be pencil. When students guess, model sounding out the phonemes so that the students can verify their prediction.

Counting Syllables

Show students various pictures of objects that they recognize. Help them to categorize the pictures by the number of "claps" (syllables) they hear when they speak this word. Words can easily be displayed in a pocket chart for all students to see or students can sort the words with word cards at their desks or in a center.

Getting the Beat

Have students listen for syllables in words by beating on a drum for each syllable or using some other percussion instrument such as a xylophone or even maracas. Older students can be asked to simply make a slight chopping motion in the air to indicate the end of each syllable as they repeat the word. Have students clap, snap, pat, rap, stomp, or tap while saying the syllables in a word. Students can also be asked to put their hands below their chins to see how many times the chin drops while saying a given word. Students can test the syllables in words they are learning as well as in their own first and last names.

Segmenting and Blending Words

Good readers parse letter strings to extract the meaning. Unlike a poor reader, the good reader does not say, "cuh-a-tuh" as separate phoneme sounds, but instead pronounces the entire one syllable of *cat* as one parsed sound. Although word recognition per se is not the goal of reading, comprehension does depend on having ready recognition of words so that short-term memory can extract meaning. Information the reader obtains from the print interacts at every level with stored knowledge to form the basis of comprehension. Unless children have a strong awareness of the phonemic structure of the English language firmly in place, asking the child the first letter or sounds of a word is to no avail. For this reason, the wise teacher begins with oral word play and word games rather than worksheets that ask students to "ring the sound" they hear.

The two most crucial skills for building solid phonemic awareness are the ability to segment words into their phonemic parts and to blend the parts into whole words (Yopp, 1988). Knowledge of segmenting words is also a predictor of success in reading (Gillet & Temple, 1990). Concentrating on developing segmenting and blending skills is more effective than a multi-skilled approach to phonemic instruction (National Institute of Child Health and Human Development, 2000). Some activities to help students learn to segment and blend phonemes include the following:

Secret Word

Students will love to play a game called "Secret Word" with other members of the class. The game can be played with partners or in small groups. Each student is given a group of cards from a deck of picture cards. The first student looks at the picture on the card in private and makes an identification of the picture. He or she then pronounces the name of the picture by stretching out the word, phoneme by phoneme, for the other students playing the game. The other students listen and try to put the sounds together fast to identify the "secret word." Students alternate turns giving the "secret word" for others in the group to guess. In a whole-class version, have students stand in a circle. Slowly pronounce the words.

Everyone is instructed to think about what the "secret word" might be. At a signal from you, the child who guessed the last word correctly gently tosses a beanbag or beach ball to another person in the circle. After the receiving person catches the tossed object, she has to "snap" the word together and tell the word as it is normally pronounced. Longer words such as *television* or *November* are good for this game.

I'm Thinking Of . . .

Play the "I'm thinking of" game by saying a word such as an animal name very slowly, sounding out each part. Students are asked to guess what you are thinking of. As students become more sophisticated with the game, have them look into a box or bag in which you have placed a special object. The student stretches out the object's name so that other students guess the identity of the mystery object.

Alphabet Wheel

Show students ending phonemes and demonstrate that changing the initial consonant can change the entire meaning of the word. Construct and demonstrate how to use an alphabet wheel with the letters from A to Z to "match" new initial consonants to the given phonemes to see if a new word they recognize can be made. For example: *bat, cat, mat, fat, hat, rat* or *ox, fox, box* or *day, hay, may, pay, ray, say, way*, etc. In a more advanced version of the game, ask students to identify words with blended phonemes to develop their skills: "br" as in *break, breakfast, bridge, brother,* etc. Students can later take similar words and make books about the words such as "I went for a walk and I saw something funny. I thought it was a . . . but it was a . . . ."

Creating New Words

Write a phoneme grouping such as "at" on an index card. Give the student individual letter pieces to place at the beginning of the word to create new words such as *bat, cat, sat,* and so forth. The same technique can also be used with initial phonemes such as "th" or "br" with students adding the endings to the words. Be sure to point out beginning, middle, and end sound positions to students as the various components are manipulated.

Identifying Beginning, Medial, and Ending Sounds

Because it is easier to distinguish beginning sounds than medial or final sounds, we should begin instruction with the beginning sounds and introduce the medial and final sounds after the child has mastered the beginning sounds. To teach the sound, select words that are one syllable in length that isolate the initial letter so that children can clearly hear the individual sound being made. Good words to use would be words similar to *cat* or *pat*, because each phoneme sound can be clearly and distinctly heard. As the word is spoken, draw out the sound of the letter being introduced so students can clearly hear the sound as it is being enunciated. Emphasis should be placed on how the phonemes feel in the mouth as they are formed. Continually draw students' attention to the position of the lips, tongue, and teeth while they are saying the sound. Students should then be asked to compare letters with very different mouth formations so that they clearly see the differences in articulation and mouth formation. Good comparison letters would be "m" and "o," for example, since the mouth is in very different positions for the formation of each letter. We should always model our own thinking aloud and ask students to frequently verbalize what they are doing so that others can also hear this information. For students who are having difficulty, provide mirrors so the students can self-monitor as they say certain words. Putting a hand in front of the lips as the word is spoken is also a helpful suggestion for students. Another strategy is to ask students to lightly touch their larynx as they pronounce different sounds so they can feel the sound that is being made. Students who lack phonemic awareness skills often try to memorize the visual aspects of a whole word. This is often what is happening when a child laboriously sounds out a word correctly but then guesses a word that is totally unrelated to the sounds that have been produced. While visual identification works for some children, for most children it is not a foundational strategy on which to build solid reading skills. Children should therefore be encouraged to continue to self-monitor their speech formations and patterns whenever possible. To help students identify beginning, medial, and ending sounds, try the following activities:

Matching Sounds

Ask students to find something in the classroom that begins with the same sound as their own name. The students say the sound that their own names begin with and then name the corresponding item that matches their initial sound. This is a good dismissal activity as students return to their seats from circle time. A more advanced version of this game is to have children match verbs with their names. An example is "Mary can march," or "Tommy can tumble."

Real or Not?

Show students a specific rime pattern such as "ing." Place individual consonant letters adjacent to the rime pattern and ask students to determine whether the newly constructed word is a real word or not. For example, placing the letter *s* with the rime pattern would produce *sing* while placing the letter *f* would produce *fing*. Emphasis should be placed on helping students understand the importance of initial sounds in making sense out of the words we hear. This is especially important for second-language learners.

Sorting Sounds

Give students a set of pictures that have two initial consonant sounds such as "c" and "r." Ask students to group the picture cards into the appropriate stack according to the initial consonant sound. Picture cards can also be sorted by medial or final sounds.

Alliterative Stories

Read alliterative stories to students stressing the alliterative sounds the author has provided. Ask students to develop sentences built around the initial sound of their own names. For example, a student named Dan might write, "Dandy Dan dallies daily during dinner." Have class challenges to see who can develop the longest, alliterative sentence. Older students can be challenged to develop whole alliterative stories.

Beginning, Middle, or End?

Give children a special snack such as crackers, gummy bears, or raisins, and two paper cups of different colors. Have students line up the cups with one color placed on the left for when they hear the sound at the beginning of the word and the other on the right for when the sound is at the end of the word. Give a word and ask children to listen for a specific sound in the word such as the sound of the letter *d*. When the "d" sound is heard at the beginning, the children place a treat in the cup on their left. If the children place the treat in the correct cup, they are allowed to eat the treat. Words that have both a beginning and ending "d" sound such as the word *dad* are even more fun as both cups get a treat at the same time. Cleanup is never a problem with this activity since children are happy to help eat the manipulatives. The game can also be played with buttons or other markers if you do not wish to use snack items during the activity.

Name Game

Sing the "Name Game" song as a line up song. As a student comes up to join the line, a rhyme is made with the "banana fana..." endings as in the song. Another version, called "Listen for the Sounds," asks students to line up if their name includes a sound. For example, if the sound given were "t", then Tim, Betty, and Brent could all line up because their names contain the sound.

Birthday Wish

Have students sit in a circle and give one student a beanbag. The student with the beanbag starts the game by saying "For my birthday, I want a _____." The other students should be listening to the final sound of the word given and thinking of an object that starts with that sound. For example, one student might say, "For my birthday, I want a bear." The student would then toss the beanbag to another student in the circle. The next student who receives the object might then say, "For my birthday, I want a radio."

Match Game

Purchase or make sets of picture cards with common objects that the students will recognize. Have students sort the picture cards into piles by the same initial or final consonant sounds. Students can also play a matching game with a matched deck of picture cards. Have students begin with a partner by laying all of the cards face down and then selecting two cards in a "match game" format. If the two cards have the same initial sound, then a "match" is made and the student gets to hold the card set. Play continues until all matches that can be made have been made.

Who Has the Card?

Pass out pictures of common objects. Play the game "Who Has the Card?" Say, "Who has the card that begins with the "d" sound and ends with the "g" sound?" The child who has the "dog" card should produce the card when it is identified. Children at higher stages of development can later be given word cards instead of picture cards and asked to play the same game by looking at the words they are holding.

Sound of the Day

For some special fun with primary students, the students or you can select a "sound of the day" to use during the day. For example, on the "t" day, students would start all of their noun words with a "t" sound instead of the letter that the word would normally start with. For example, say "took" instead of book or "tarry" instead of "Mary." Students will have fun trying to match the special sound of the day to the nouns they use around the classroom that day.

Listen, Listen

Help students look at words and isolate the sounds or phonemes that they hear in various parts of a word. For example, "Listen for words that start with the sound of "m." Have students raise their hands as they hear the "m" sound in a story that you read to the class. Waxed pipe cleaner strands can also be used to ring the special letters on the big book page as the class listens to the material. The same strategy can also be used for medial or final sounds or any other special features you want to point out to students.

Word Boundaries

As students write sentences, ask them to use a different color crayon to write each word on their paper. This will help them think about the boundaries for each word as they are writing the word.

What's My Label?

Labels around the room help students link objects with the concept of a word. Point to the labels and help students read the word labels and identify the object that matches the label.

One to One

Draw horizontal dash lines on a paper or on the overhead to represent the sounds that students hear in a word. Push pennies, buttons, or paper clips into the line spaces as each sound is said so that students see a representation of the sound as it is made. After students have mastered the basic level of this activity, they can move to more complex forms where they are asked to compare the lengths of two words as they push their manipulatives into the line spaces. An even more advanced version of this activity can also be done. Ask students to use their manipulatives to signal syllables for longer words in a given sentence. This is a good activity to practice after students have grasped the concept of phonemes in words.

Developing the Concept of Words

One of the crucial understandings that beginning readers need to develop is the concept of a "word" as a collection of sounds that together provide meaning. Students need to understand that while a few words consist of a single phoneme, most words contain more than one phoneme. They also need to learn that words come in various lengths and that they can be organized into sentences that together give a message. When young students first begin to write, they often do not understand the idea that spaces separate words, so they run all of their words together on the page. Teachers often offer the suggestion that children place a finger on the paper before writing the next word to help them understand that words have space boundaries. The more students are exposed to playing with words, the sooner they will develop understandings around words. Some ideas to help students examine words follow:

Counting Words

Give students a sentence and have them match counters with the number of words they see in the short sentence. Counters can be either nonedible such as buttons or plastic chips or edible such as raisins, grapes, or crackers. The children can place beans or buttons into a cup as the words in the sentences are indicated.

Building Sentences

Display several sentences in a pocket chart with a blank pocket above each sentence. Make duplicates of the sentences and cut them up into their individual words. Give each group of students one set of words that makes up one of the sentences in the pocket chart. Students must put the individual words into the proper order and then place them correctly above the sentence that corresponds to the sentence they are reconstructing. This activity can also be a good one for children to do as a center activity on their own.

Same or Different?

Show students two words with one written above the other. Ask students to compare the letters in each word and to decide if the words are the same or different. Example: Compare *mouse* with *house*. Compare *run* with *run*. Compare *want* with *went*. Ask students to describe what is different about the words if they think they are different. Ask, "How do you know?"

Word Thoughts

Play a game with students called "I'm thinking of a word." Give students clues to help them identify the word. For example, "I am thinking of a word that ends in 'ice' and are small, furry animals that like cheese." Picture cards can also be used to show students that their guesses are correct or incorrect. A variation of this game is to give the entire word by the elongated phoneme components (such as /m/i/suh for the word mice) and then ask students to consolidate the phonemes and guess the word. Students can also play "What's in my birthday package?" by listening to elongated words to guess the mystery item. This game can also be played with a box by asking, "What do I have in the box?"

What Doesn't Belong?

Students can play "What doesn't belong?" by being shown three picture cards with the same phoneme components. One word should be different from the featured phonemes so students can identify the word that doesn't belong. After each word, ask the student to explain why it does not belong with the other two words in the group.

Developing the Concepts of Print

During the early stages of phonemic awareness, it is also desirable to help students begin to understand the concepts of print. Students need to understand that print conveys meaning. They also need to understand how print is processed, how we interpret the symbols on the page, and how a book is read by the reader. To help students develop these associations, point out and model the various components for the students as they listen to a book being read. According to Marie Clay (1993), some understandings that we would want students to develop at this stage include the following:

• Readers begin reading at the left of the line of print and progress across the page to the right.

• A return sweep of the eyes is made to the next line of print at the left side of the page.

• Readers begin reading at the top of the page and work downward on the page.

• Readers begin at the front of the book and read to the back of the book.

The following activities will help students develop an understanding of the concepts of print.

Special Student of the Day

Place all of the children's names in a hat and draw one name out each day. This child becomes the "Kindergartner of the Day" or "1st Grader of the Day." As a result, the child gets to do special things all throughout his or her "special day," such as sit in a special chair, be the line leader, or be the messenger. Write a class poem or story about the student of the day. Students can help you create each sentence by suggesting where to start, what letter to start with, what letter comes next, and so forth. After the message is written, ask students to help you analyze the sounds and letters in the message. Have the "student of the day" point to the words with a pointer as the class reads back the story. Leave the writing on the chart stand during the day so that other students have an opportunity to come up and use the pointer to read the story themselves. At the end of the day, the special student takes the poem or story home. The stories about each child can also be typed and placed into a book. A digital picture of each child can complete the page. The book should be laminated, spiral bound, and placed in the student reading center for all to enjoy.

Featured Books

Using a big book version of a story that all students can see, lead a discussion with students on the title, cover art, and illustrations of the book. Invite students to predict the storyline, and then read the story to the students, stopping at key points to ask for predictions. On a subsequent lesson, ask students to retell the story from looking at the pictures. Use the same book to highlight different word structures or patterns. Cover word parts with sticky notes and ask students to predict what word is under the sticky note. Have children join in the rereading either chorally or in small groups. After several books have been used in this way, ask students to choose which book will be "featured" for the day. If possible, have smaller versions of the big books available in the free reading areas for children to reread on their own during the remainder of the day.

Building Books

Construct alphabet books by asking students to draw pictures for each letter using themes such as space, hobbies and games, or animals. Students will enjoy looking at the books over and over again. This is also a great way to build a collection of inexpensive big books that children will love to read and reread.

Finding Patterns

Find books, songs, and poems that have rhyme, alliteration, or assonance. Point out the unique patterns that the material contains as the text is read. Even when children cannot yet read the words themselves, use a pointer with big books to "follow along" with the words as they are being read from the book. Ask children to complete pages for a book with a simple sentence and an illustration that matches the sentence. Some books that might be made are alphabet books, or books on topics such as "things in the room," "things I like to eat," "people who are important to us," and "animals we like."

Parents and early primary teachers must help students discover the richness of language by surrounding children early in life with as much language and oral richness as possible. As children see print and hear adults make associations between the spoken word and symbols on the page, children will begin to recognize that there is a relationship between the symbols they see on the page and the spoken sounds they hear. By listening to a large number of stories where words are used in creative ways and by "playing with words" through rhymes, poems, riddles, songs, finger plays, and games, children can fine tune their phonemic awareness skills. With a solid foundation of phonemic awareness, children will be able to build a tight weave with the other threads of reading.

Developing a Sense of Rhythm and Rhyme

Another way to foster a child's fascination with print is by extensive reading of books that have a strong sense of rhythm, pattern, and predictability. Developing a sense of rhythm is beneficial to learning to read.

Researchers from the University College in London. (Goswami, et al., 2002) found that children who read very well for their age had a strong ability to spot rhythms and beats. Children with dyslexia had difficulty identifying the rime in words such as *fit* and *fat*. Researchers concluded that an awareness of beat and rhythm could influence the way children process speech patterns. This in turn, can affect their reading and writing skills. Training in rhyme and beat can help develop this distinction in young children as their reading skills emerge.

Nursery rhymes, chants, songs, poetry, and predictable print books all have the types of patterns necessary for building strong talk-print linkages. Teachers in grades K–1 should often use books that contain either predictable pictures or predictable word patterns. Use "sticky notes" to cover a predictable word and ask students to guess the hidden word. This strategy will help students develop strong decoding and prediction skills. Dr. Seuss books, ABC books, or repetitive books such as Bill Martin's *Brown Bear, Brown Bear* (1970) or Margaret Weis Brown's *Goodnight Moon* (1947) are also helpful for teaching a sense of rhythm and pattern. More complex books should also be read so that children continue to expand their vocabulary and sense of language development.

Phonemic awareness activities should be short, fast paced, varied, and, above all, fun for the children. We should choose books that are well written and clearly illustrated. At the beginning, the books should not have too much print so that students can learn to "read along with" the reader as the story is read to them. Strong repetitive patterns that stress rhyming words, such as Dr. Seuss' *There's a Wocket in My Pocket* (1996) are good choices to use at this level. Another strategy is to take "picture walks" through the book prior to reading the book for the first time. Ask children to make predictions based on the pictures about what might happen in the story. After reading for enjoyment, have children play with the language and even act out portions of the story. Try the following techniques to help children develop a sense of rhythm and rhyme:

Rhymes and Rhythms

Use a big book, such as *Mrs. Wishy-Washy* (1987) by Joy Cowley, with a specific rhyme pattern featured throughout the book. Have students listen to the rhymes and identify the rhyming word sounds. Students can also be asked to make predictions about what words might be used in each sentence. Stop to recap and highlight rhymes with students on a frequent basis. The more it is put in an enjoyable, game-like context, the more students will enjoy finding rhymes and rhythms.

Rotating Rhymes

Help students develop a strong sense of rhyme and pattern by reading repetitive or predictable stories chorally. For example, students in half of the class would read with you, "There was an old woman who lived in a shoe" and the second half of the class would then read, "She had so many children she didn't know what to do." Rotation continues throughout the story with the class switching parts. The children will love being active participants in the reading of the story.

What's Different?

Read familiar nursery rhymes or short stories to the children but change something about the sentences as they are read. For example, "the moon jumped over the cow" (reverse words); "little boy green" (substitute words); "Mary had a little ram" (change the consonants); "little Miss Tuffet sat on a muffet" (change the sequence or order of events in the story). Children should be listening attentively to spot the problems. When they identify a problem, they should be asked to explain why it is incorrect and what the correct response should be. This game sharpens student's awareness of phonology, words, syntax, semantics, and listening attentiveness.

Writing Helps Establish Strong Phonemic Awareness Connections

Writing is important to developing strong phonemic awareness skills. Inventive spelling provides us with much insight into the development of a child's phonemic understanding. Morris and Perney (1984) have identified four stages of spelling development in children: pre-phonemic, phonemic, transitional, and correct spelling. Children begin their writing attempts as pre-phonemic spellers. In this stage, spellers perceive and represent initial and final consonants by one-syllable words, often using letter names to represent phonemes. For example, the child might write *j, js,* or *jc* for the word *dress.* Children who advance to the phonemic stage begin to use short vowels as phonologically appropriate substitutions. For example, the child might write *sek* for *sink* or *fet* for *feet.* Spellers in the transitional stage begin to represent short vowels correctly, but the vowel markers may be incorrectly placed such as *sied* for *side.* Correct spelling is when the child nearly always spells the words in the conventional manner when writing.

As children become more proficient writers, they often go through a period of time when they reject inventive spelling and insist on writing a word the "right way" (Sulzby, 1996). This too is a characteristic of children who are about to move from the transitional stage to the correct spelling stage.

We can also help develop the link between oral and written language by creating shared writings around a common theme. An example is to make a chart or an illustrated student-authored big book using the starters "I can . . ." or "I like . . ." or a similar sentence stem. Students add their own ending and the class chorally reads and practices the writing. Students can be asked to reflect on what they "notice" in the writing that they are reading. Writing as much as possible, even when students are still at the "scribble" stage, helps build a strong sense of phonemic awareness.

Weaving the Thread of Phonemic Awareness

When children have phonemic awareness they understand that the sounds of spoken language fit together to make words and that those words convey meaning. Beginning readers must learn that reading is the process of acquiring meaning from text. There are many skills that children must learn as they begin to make sense of the various symbols and arrangements of words and letters. They need to understand the connection between the sounds that they hear in everyday language and the letters that they see on a page. They also need to understand how sounds fit together to form words and they must be able to manipulate the various parts of words and syllables to create new words. They need to understand how print is processed and that books and writing can be wonderful sources of knowledge and entertainment in their lives. With solid phonemic awareness skills, students are then ready to begin formal instruction in phonics.

✣ 2 ✣

Phonics and Decoding

The second thread of reading instruction involves phonics and decoding. Phonics is the ability to identify that there is a relationship between the individual sounds (phonemes) of the spoken language and the letters (graphemes) of the written language. Decoding is being able to use visual, syntactic, or semantic cues to make meaning from words and sentences. Visual cues are how the word looks, the letters themselves, and the letter combinations or groupings and their associated sounds. Syntactic cues are how the sentences are structured and how the words are ordered. Semantic cues are how the word fits into the context of the sentence as in the part of speech, the association with pictures, or the meaning cues in the sentence.

Students must learn that there are systematic and predictable relationships between letter combinations and spoken sound. While formal phonics instruction is important, it should not take up more than 25 percent of available reading instruction time. Students should be engaged in actual reading much more than they are engaged in discussing the act of reading (Allington, 2001). Phonics should be a strong component of all kindergarten and 1st grade instruction so that students build strong word attack skills as a foundation for all of their reading skills. Instruction should consist of a planned sequence of instruction taught in a systematic way. While there are many commercial phonics programs available for consideration, it is important that teachers in a school choose one consistent method or approach for phonics instruction so that everyone is continuing to reinforce the same strategies and techniques in the same manner with the students. An ordered, sequential program that examines all phonics components is one of the keys to successful student achievement in this thread.

What Should Be Taught During Phonics Instruction?

Instruction in phonics involves helping beginning readers learn how sounds are linked to letters and letter combinations in the written language. It teaches that there is a predictable pattern to much of our language. Once phonics skills are mastered, students will be able to decipher words encountered in reading and spell the various words they wish to write. When students are focusing less on decoding, they can spend more attention on making meaning from the print they are reading.

Phonics should be heavily emphasized in early grades so as to develop a solid foundation for more advanced decoding skills (National Institute of Child Health and Human Development, 2000). Phonics instruction is not a panacea for teaching all students to read but the majority of students can be helped to learn to read and spell more effectively with the introduction of phonics in the beginning reading stages. Older readers may well have other issues beyond decoding that interfere with efficient reading so simply providing training in phonics may not solve a struggling reader's problems.

Children should be aware of what they are learning and how knowing sound-symbol correspondences will help them become better readers. They should be taught to use phoneme letter and sound combinations as they directly manipulate words and sentences. Phoneme combinations should not be presented in isolation but should be directly applicable to a child's reading. Instruction should link prior knowledge with new learning and should be systematic, ordered, and deliberate.

Phonics instruction should be limited to one or two types of manipulation at a time to give children a chance to master the concepts presented. Juel and Roper-Schneider (1985) found that children were better able to use their phonics knowledge to improve decoding as well as comprehension when the texts they were reading contained a high percentage of words that followed the patterns introduced by the teacher. Teach either phonics concepts that will be identified as "strategies" that children can use in their general reading practice or find materials that conform to the specific patterns being presented to students. There are many commercially available "controlled" books that limit the phonic patterns presented to specific structures, so finding materials should not be a problem. In any case, students must be able to apply the skills they are learning to context. This will allow them to apply the direct instruction they have received and will cement their learning.

A suggestion for introducing phonics sounds to students is to begin by reading a story that contains a specific phonic element such as the short "a" sound in a story. An example of a story that fits this element is *Angus and the Cat* by Marjorie Flack (1985). Follow this by another book that reinforces the same concept of the short "a" sound such as *The Cat in the Hat* by Dr. Seuss (1957). This concept of short "a" introduced and applied immediately to active reading helps students develop a solid understanding of the phoneme being presented. Students should then be allowed to practice reading simple passages or books that have this same concept so that they continue to apply the new understanding in direct context. Controlled vocabulary books at their reading level are good for this purpose during the practice stage but students should not be restricted to these materials for all of their reading experiences. Pressley et al. (1998) noted that in the most effective classrooms, students not only had skill instruction provided but also were immersed in literature and writing, with "virtually every day filled with exposure to and reading of excellent literature and writing" (p. 16).

An Effective Phonics Lesson

Phonics lessons should be well ordered and sequential. They should be fast-paced, multi-modal, fun, and very focused. A good phonics program will contain instruction on phonemes, individual letters as well as blends, sound combinations, and other linguistic structures. It will also build on patterns within onsets and rimes within the words examined. (The "onset" is all letters of the word up to the vowel, and the "rime" is the vowel and letters after the vowel.) An effective phonics lesson should concentrate on linking what students already know with new information and should emphasize decoding in context rather than learning rules in isolation. Decoding must always be coupled with meaning and "sense-making," because without comprehension, true reading has not taken place.

Teachers should begin letter introduction by presenting two letters that are very different graphically so that students can make comparisons. For example, we might introduce the letter "t" and the letter "m" because they require different mouth, teeth, lip, and tongue positions. Taking time to have students feel the difference and tying the letters to concrete experiences (like animal names and kinesthetic movements or signals) will help the students imprint the learning into their minds. Teachers can help students link words they know to these same sounds so they can develop an association with the sounds and the words. Some examples of questions (Stanovich, 1993, Stanovich & Siegel, 1994) that a teacher might ask students during instruction are:

- Phoneme Deletion: What would be left if the "t'" sound were removed from the word *tug*?

- Word to Word Matching: Do *hog* and *hat* begin with the same sound?

- Blending: What word would we have if you put together the sounds "c", "a", "t"?

- Phoneme Segmentation: What sounds do you hear in the word *top*?

- Phoneme Counting: How many sounds do you hear in the word *lamb*?

- Deleted Phoneme: What sound do you hear in *stop* that is missing in *top*?

- Odd Word Out: Which word starts with a different sound: *sand, sack, lake,* or *sandwich*?

- Sound to Word Matching: Is there a /t/ sound in the word *little*?

Phonics concepts that should be taught directly to students include

- Single consonants.
- Initial consonant blends: "bl," "br," "cl," "cr," "dr," "fl," "fr," "gl," "gr," "pl," "pr," "sc," "sch," "sk," "sl," "sm," "sn," "sp," "spr," "st," "str," "sw," and "tr."
- Final consonant blends: "ld," "lf," "lk," "nce," "nk," and "nt."
- Consonant digraphs (two letters that make up one sound): "ch," "gh," "kn," "ph," "sc," "sh," "th," "wh," and "wr."
- Long and short vowels.
- Vowel digraphs: "ai," "au," "ay," "ee," "ea," "oa," "oi," "ou," "ow," and "oy."
- "R" controlled vowel patterns: "ar," "ark," "art," "are," "ear," "ert," "irl," "url," "urn," "orn," "ort," and "ore."

Phonics Programs and Systematic Instruction

Phonics concepts should be presented in a systematic, hierarchical order from easier concepts to more difficult ones as the child's skill develops. Adequate time should be allowed for the child to master one set of skills and understandings before moving on to the next group. Understanding what students have mastered and what they need to work on is vital to the instructional planning process.

There are many commercial phonics programs available for purchase that are systematic and implicit in their approach. A highly tactile and kinesthetic approach that connects known content (such as animals) to a sound and an associated kinesthetic movement to each letter of the alphabet and phoneme group may help young students build solid links in a fun and engaging way. Brain researchers uniformly assert that the more links the brain has on any given piece of learning, the more solid the concept is in our memory. This applies to beginning readers as well, so care should be taken to select a commercial phonics program that addresses as many of the learning modalities as possible. Skilled, well-trained teachers may also develop their own phonics programs to use within the context of literature shared in the classroom. In any case, the program should systematically introduce all concepts and reinforce them at strategic points for optimum retention. The following activities might help teach basic phonics concepts:

Flash Cards

Make up or purchase decks of flash cards with letters that commonly appear together such as "ay" or "ch" or "bl." Have students quiz one another on the sounds that these letter combinations make. If possible, ask students to also give a word that contains this letter combination. This activity can also be played as a whole class or used in a learning center as a choice in the center menu.

Which Word Doesn't Belong?

Select two words that have the same initial sound and one word that does not have the same sound. Mix the order of the three words. Carefully say each word for students, emphasizing and elongating the initial sound that is heard in each word. Ask students to identify the words that have the same initial consonant sound and which word does not belong with the other two. This can also be done using the overhead projector or a pocket chart.

Letter Bingo

Make bingo cards with initial letter sounds. Show students pictures and say the name of the object. Ask students to think about what letter the picture begins with and to cover that letter on their bingo card. Play continues until a student has a "bingo" according to the regular rules of the game. When a child believes that he has a bingo, the letters are read back by both their letter name as well as at least one way that the letter is pronounced. Check the called words and verify the bingo.

Stretch and Snap

Students need to develop an understanding of how to break down a word into its component sounds, but this is often not enough for them to recognize the word. In order to recognize a word, students need to make the association between the sounds and how they fit together to form a word. Teach students to s—*tr*—*e*—*t*—*ch* a word out by its sounds and then to *snap* the word back together to aide them in oral recognition of the word. Frequent practice of this technique will help students identify words that stump them while reading.

Same or Different

Give each student two cards, one with the word *same* written on it and one with the word *different*. Then say two words such as *pair* and *pain* or *pen* and *pen* to the students. After each word pair, ask students to hold up the card that corresponds to whether the words are the same or different from each other. Keep a watchful eye for students who often do not display the correct card. They may need more intensive phonics work on sound discrimination.

Reading Log

Ask students to keep a reading log of how they solved problems in decoding while reading. Have the students write down precisely where they encountered the problem. They should also record the strategy that they used to approach the word and how it worked. Examine these logs and help students think about which strategies were most successful. Reflecting on successes will help students identify the strategies that work so they can use them again in more independent situations. This strategy works better for older readers.

Word Maker

Divide paper or plastic plates into several segments with a permanent marker. Write various word-ending phonograms into the divided segments of the paper plate. Place beginning parts of words on clothespins. Ask students to match beginning parts of a word with endings to create a word by attaching the clothespin to the paper plate. Place the answers on the back of the plate so the students can easily check their accuracy by themselves. This activity makes a good "center" activity for young students.

Missing Letter

Using laminated letter cards, place letters on the chalkboard tray with a blank card indicating a missing letter in some location of the word. Show students a concrete object and provide the name of the object. Ask students to come to the front of the class and select the correct letter card that will spell the word of the object shown. This can also be done on the overhead by leaving a line for the missing letter. Students can come to the overhead and write the missing letter into the space.

Blending Letters

Primary students can work together to form words. Make laminated letter cards with at least three of each letter and six of more common letters and vowels. Punch holes in the top of each card and put string through the holes so that students can wear their letters around their necks. Give a small group of students several letter cards and ask them to make a word to show to the rest of the class by organizing themselves in the proper order. For a more advanced version, ask the class if anyone has a letter that can change the word to become a new word. If so, the new child comes up to replace the letter that is no longer needed. The word is again sounded out so that all students can see and hear the word that has been made. In more sophisticated versions of the game, blends or digraphs can also be introduced into the letter card set and letters can be added to change the word into a longer word. For example, the name *Stan* can be changed to *stand* with the addition of the letter *d.*

Hangman

Play hangman with students. Hints such as the beginning letter or the ending letter of the word can also be given to assist students in guessing the missing letters of the mystery word. Take this a step further by showing on the overhead or whiteboard sentences with one or two missing "mystery words." Cover the mystery word with sticky notes for each letter or leave blanks in the sentence indicating the number of letters of the word. Write in the letters identified as students "guess" the missing letters of the mystery word. This game not only helps students examine the letter patterns of the word but also encourages them to use context clues to identify words that might fit into the sentence.

Word Hopscotch

Place initial letters and pattern blends on the floor in a grid format using colored masking tape or book tape. Ask students to hop through the board by jumping from letter to letter and saying the word that has been created with the jump sequence that is selected. For example, put the letters "*b*," "*t*," "*p*" in the first row, "*a*," "*o*," "i," in the second row and "*t*," "*p*," "*m*" in the third row.

Rhyme and Syllabification

Understanding the concepts of rhyme and syllabification is important to a beginning reader. Students need to develop an understanding of the concepts of word and rhyme, as well as the ability to rhyme words, segment syllables, and hear the onset and rimes in words (Treiman & Zukowski, 1991). Once they have mastered these skills, students can then learn to separate words into individual phonemes and also to blend phonemes back into real words. These skills are also foundational skills for building solid reading abilities in young students.

When adults read, they do not refer to a set of rules—so simply having students learn a specific set of phonics rules does not necessarily translate into improved reading ability. Adult readers recognize new words by comparing the patterns in unknown words to spelling patterns in words they already know (Adams, 1990). Adults often look for prefixes, suffixes, or root words that they recognize to assist in the decoding process. Fluent readers often separate unknown words into two types of patterns, onsets and rimes. The "onset" is all letters of the word up to the vowel, and the "rime" is the vowel and letters after the vowel. Effective decoders analyze patterns in new words to assist in word recognition as they read. Phonics instruction helps children develop this strategy. Children need to learn to recognize word parts and letter groups. They must make a connection between the letter groups they see with the pronunciations they know for those onsets and rimes. They must then be able to recombine the sounds into a word that they can recognize from their listening and speaking vocabulary. For older readers who seem to be having difficulty with decoding, linking rhyme patterns to unlocking the identity of words can be the missing link they need to improve their decoding skills.

Helping students learn to process rhyme patterns is not difficult. Nearly 500 words can be derived from only 37 rime patterns (Wylie and Durrell, 1970). These rime segments should be taught to children to help improve their reading and writing vocabulary because they lend themselves to so many words in the child's vocabulary. The 37 common rimes are *ack, ain, ake, ale, all, ame, an, ank, ap, ash, at, ate, aw, ay, eat, ell, est, ice, ick, ide, ight, ill, in, ine, ing, ink, ip, ir, ock, oke, op, or, ore, uck, ug, ump,* and *unk.* Once students understand how to use the concepts of onset and rime to unlock the pronunciation of a word, they can then be taught to use context clues to make meaning out of the sentence they are reading. For example, if the child knows the word *pain* and applies the same "ain" pronunciation to the word *drain,* then context can be used to read the sentence, "The plumber unclogged the *drain* and let the water flow out of the sink." Using rimes guide word meaning is helpful to both comprehension and decoding (Cunningham, 1991). Whenever working at this level, we must be sure to continue linking the sounds to the actual meaning of words themselves so that comprehension is the final result of any segmenting or sounding out of word parts. While decoding is important, the goal is comprehension of what is being read, not just the decoding of the words. Without this link, some children become excellent "word callers" but have no comprehension of the text that they have just read.

The optimum time for a heavy emphasis on phonics instruction is during the kindergarten and 1st grade years so that children develop solid word attack skills from the beginning of their introduction to reading. Children who do not receive this instruction during the optimum time frame may miss out on key elements and understandings and may need remediation later on. Remediation for older readers however, is much more complex than when students are just beginning to learn how to read and different strategies will need to be applied than simply learning phonics concepts. Some ways to reinforce the understanding of rhyme and syllabification are:

Word Tic Tac Toe

Teach students a twist on the familiar game of tic tac toe by using words that contain two featured sounds instead of "x" and "o". Each player selects a different sound to use during play. At each turn, students must write a word that has the targeted sound in an empty space on the board. The first student to write three words in a row that follow the given criteria is the winner just as in the traditional game.

Word Lists

Ask students to work in teams or with partners to develop lists of words that sound the same at the beginning, middle, or end, as directed. Give a time limit and see how many words are written within this time frame. Early primary teachers can do this as a class with the teacher writing the words on the chalkboard or on poster paper as students brainstorm.

Trait Analysis

Have students examine a given passage for examples of several specific traits that have been identified for the students. For example: Find all of the words with the short "i" sound or the long "o" sound. Have students highlight the different words if possible and then prepare a graph to show how many words contained each trait that was analyzed. Words can also be placed on Venn diagrams to show their commonalities.

Detective Teams

To work with the hard and soft sounds of letters like "c" and "g," divide students into "detective teams" of three or four players. Each player is given either the soft or hard sound and asked to brainstorm as many words as possible that begin with this sound. At the end of a short time period, lists are compared. Make a list of the words under each sound to see how many unique words the students have been able to find during the given time. Students should list all of the rhyming words they find that match the ending given.

Blending Letters

To help students understand the concept of blending letters to form a word, display a large play slide on a pocket chart or on the wall. Use sticky notes with the individual phonemes and display them from top to bottom on the slide. Show students how the letters slide down the slide together as a group to form the blended word at the bottom of the slide (Johns & Lenski, 2001). Ask students to blend new words with letter tiles and their own paper slides at their desks.

Rhyming Pairs

Make a deck of "Rhyming Pairs" on three-by-five-inch cards and distribute to students in the class. Each student must locate the person who has a word that rhymes with the word on his or her own card. Have each student pair locate two additional items in the room that rhyme with the words on their cards. Each partner group should share their four rhyming words with the class.

Word Baseball

Divide the class into two teams. Display a card with a high-frequency word on it. If the student can read the word, he or she goes to "first base." If the child can give a rhyming word, he or she goes to "second base," and if the child can give another word that has the same initial sound as the given word, the student goes to third base. If the student can give a word that contains the same vowel sound as the given word it is a "homerun." If the student misses reading the word, it is an "out" for the team. If the child misses any other level, he or she remains "on base." The game can be played for as many innings as desired.

Magnetic Board

Provide students with a magnetic board and plastic magnetic letters to use as manipulatives. Help students get a better feel for spelling patterns and syllable combinations by asking students to make given words on the magnetic board with the letters. Students can even make sentences on the magnetic board if enough letters are available.

Word Bank

Give students a set of words that have many rhyming word matches. Then give the students a set of words to categorize under each rhyme set. A game that can be played with this word bank is to give a sentence with a missing word. The children look at the word bank words and select the missing word to write on their paper or on an overhead transparency.

Go Fish

Write sight words (two of each word) on a deck of three-by-five-inch cards and deal 5 or 6 cards to each player. Students have to ask for the mate to their card by describing it phonetically. For example, to match a card with the word "bee" the student might say, "Do you have a card that has a long 'e' sound and rhymes with *tree*?" If the player being asked does not have such a card, he or she responds with "Go fish!" and the child takes a card from the deck.

Sorting by Patterns

Give students a stack of word cards with high-frequency words written on them. Ask students to sort the cards by patterns such as words with long "a," words with short "a," "r" controlled vowels, words ending in the same suffix, and so forth. This helps students recognize patterns and categorize the sounds they hear in words.

Rhyming Couplets

Show children a rhyming couplet and then let them work in small groups to write additional couplets to go with the original rhyme provided. Ask students to be creative in adding stanzas that help make the rhyme a funny poem at the end.

Word Ladders

Ask the students to make a "word ladder" as long as possible by changing the next word in line by just one letter. For example, the word given might be *fat*. Students would first change the "t" to "r" to make the word *far*. They could then change the "f" to "t" to make the word *tar*. Students are encouraged to build as long a word ladder as possible in a given amount of time.

In with the In Crowd

Give students a list of three or four words that are in the group and another list of words that are out of the group based on a common feature. As you give new words, the students must decide if the word is "in" or "out" based on what they think the criteria of the grouping might be. The word is added to the proper column and play continues with a new word. When students can identify the special feature of the "in group," the game ends. A bit of competition can be added between teacher and student by only allowing students to make a specific number of guesses. If the correct answer is determined prior to the guess limit, the students win the game. If no answer is given by the end of the clues, the teacher wins. The students will enjoy challenging you in this manner. Categories can be anything you want to feature, including words with silent "e," palindromes, one-syllable words, compound words, and prepositions. Students can also teach this game to their families to play at home. This game promotes analysis and causes students to deeply examine common features of words.

Patterns Are Important to Decoding

Patterns are also helpful ways of learning to decode words. Two patterns that should be introduced to students are:

- Onset: the initial part of the word that precedes the vowel. For example, in the word *top*, the "t" would be the onset. In the word *snake*, the "sn" would be the onset.

- Rime: the vowel and the letters that follow in a word. For example, in the word *batch*, the "atch" would be the rime and would form the basis for different rhymes such as *snatch, match, hatch,* and *catch.*

When students learn the rime patterns, it can help unlock the pronunciation of many more words that contain the same rime pattern. It is also helpful to have students in 2nd and 3rd grades examine syllabification rules. These rules, while not necessarily helpful for reading, will assist the students in their writing. Some rules that students might find helpful are:

- When a syllable ends in a vowel, the vowel is long, as in *ivy*.
- When a syllable ends in a consonant, the vowel is short, as in *apple*.
- Divide a word between two like consonants, as in *lit-tle*.
- Divide a word between two unlike consonants, as in *sen-tence*.
- When a consonant comes between two vowels, divide after the first vowel, as in *mu-sic*.
- Prefixes, suffixes, and inflectional endings are always syllables.

Manipulating Words

Students also need to study words and how words fit together. Some specific patterns that should be taught include compound words, contractions, plurals, prefixes, affixes, root words, suffixes, homophones, homographs, and alliteration patterns in words that start with the same sounds. There are many activities that can help students look at words and the manipulation of words, including the following ideas.

Sentence Construction

Assist students in creating several sentences that are written on the board or placed on sentence strips and displayed in a pocket chart. Make a second set of the same sentences and cut these into individual words. For primary students, punch holes in the top of the card and put a string through the holes so each child can wear a word. Visitor clip-on badges also work well for older students. Ask students to find other students in the room who have words that fit into their sentence. When they have located all of the pieces of their sentence and matched their words to the original sentence, the students should indicate that they are ready for an adult to check their work. This is a fun way for students to notice word order as well as the characteristics of a sentence. A more advanced version of this activity would place the punctuation for the sentence on cards as well and ask students to find the punctuation that applies to their sentence and add the person to their sentence group.

Little Words

Encourage children to examine words and identify the "little words" they find inside of larger words. Students should be encouraged to find words inside of words to make them more aware of how letter groups work together to make one sound.

Prefixes and Suffixes

Teach children in 3rd grade and higher to recognize prefixes and suffixes to help unlock word meanings. For example, if students know that the prefix "dis" means *not*, it will help them unlock the meanings of words such as *disbelief* or *disappear,* and many others. Have students find lists of words that contain the targeted prefix and show how the prefix helps to make the meaning of the base word change. Show students how adding or removing prefixes can help unlock the meaning of many words they come across in their reading.

Identifying Words

Write sight words on flash cards. Play a game with a small group of students by seeing who can recognize and "win" the card the quickest. This strategy helps develop fluency as well as sight-word recognition because speed is involved. Be sure readers are fairly evenly matched, however, so the competitive aspect of the game does not become the focal point of the activity. Cards can also be displayed to individual students in a small group in round-robin fashion. The student is asked to identify the word or to "pass" the card on to the next student if he cannot identify it. The student identifying the word collects the card. Again, be sure students are fairly matched in ability so the focus is on reading the word, not on "winning" cards or competing against other students.

Matching Words

Make a matching card game by making two cards of each sight word. Deal seven cards to each player and then have students take turns drawing cards from each other and making matches. As the match is made, the player who made the match must read the matching words out loud. If the player cannot read the words, the cards are put in a special "discard pile," not in the player's card collection. The player with the most card matches at the end of the deck can be the "winner" for a touch of competition to the game, if desired.

Sentence Assembly

Ask students to create a complete sentence (or several sentences for older students). Cut the sentence into individual words and ask the student to reassemble the words in the correct order. For multiple sentences, ask students to find all of the additional sentences that can be made from the available words. This is a particularly helpful strategy for non-English speakers who need to learn the syntax of the English language.

Storyboard

Cut comic strips from the newspaper or cut old picture books apart. Mix the frames and have students put the story back into proper order using the syntactical cues and story events. A "wordless story" can also be used, and students can be asked to write the narratives for each frame. Have students explain their thinking on why they ordered the story frames as they did.

Compound Words

Ask groups of students to find compound words that fit into various categories such as people, things, places, and times. See which group can think of the most compound words. A more advanced version of this activity would be to have students also develop riddles around the compound words.

Word Dominoes

Create compound-word dominoes by writing a word on the top and a word on the bottom of three-by-five-inch cards. Students play dominoes with the word cards by matching words that can make a compound word.

Flash Cards for Compound Words

Younger children can examine compound words by making compound word flash cards. Students begin by folding a piece of paper so that there are two flaps coming together evenly on the top. The student then prints a compound word on the interior of a paper, and writes each separate word on one side of the flap to visually break apart the two words by lifting the flaps. Students can illustrate the compound word on the bottom part of the flash card as well as the meanings of the individual words when they stand independently to show how the meaning changes. The visual representation helps students to understand that words can have different meanings when combined and that longer words are sometimes made up of smaller words.

Cloze Passages

Cloze passages where key words are omitted and students have to fill in the blanks are a good way to help readers develop the ability to predict what words might make sense in a sentence. Take a passage and eliminate fairly predictable words. Students must use context clues to try to fill in the blanks with words that makes sense in the story. This helps students develop their skills in predicting and anticipating meaning while reading. Any guess that makes sense in the context of the sentence is acceptable even if it not the word from the original passage.

Missing Punctuation

Being able to examine and correctly place punctuation in writing is an essential skill to decoding. In this activity, write a short poem or passage on the board or chart paper and then ask students to help fill in the missing punctuation so the passage can be properly read. This activity helps students understand phrasing and sentence construction. The activity can even be used for older children with the introduction of complex and compound-complex sentences and more advanced forms of punctuation such as colons and semicolons. Students should be asked to explain why the various punctuations are correct in the given position and why other forms of punctuation would not be correct. In some cases, more than one interpretation might be possible. Ask students to describe the differences in meaning reflective of the different positions of the punctuation.

Organization

Understanding the organization of a piece of writing is one of the keys to learning to decode effectively. Students should be able to identify the introduction, body, and conclusion in a passage of nonfiction. They should be able to identify the lead, development, rising action, conflict, plot climax, and resolution in fictional material. Have students examine various pieces of writing and identify the key elements.

Jeopardy

Use classroom word walls to make a game of "Jeopardy." Students are placed into teams and can guess the words on the basis of the clues just like on the television version of the Jeopardy game. For example, the clue for the word *book* might say, "something one can read." Points are given just as in the real game with the higher points given for harder clues. The game can be played by individuals or teams. When the team version is played, students on each team may discuss the answer but only the designated spokesperson can give the answer for the group.

Nouns

Students need to understand how nouns play an important part in a story. Ask students to write a short story in a rebus format. Students can either draw pictures or use stickers to replace key nouns in the story. Older students can create rebus stories for young children who have not learned to read. The younger children can assist the reader by supplying the noun that fits the picture in the story.

How Can Miscue Analysis Help in Phonics Instruction?

A quick way to assess what students know and do not know is to administer an "oral reading record" or "running record" (Clay, 1972) to the student and carefully mark all of the mistakes or hesitations made on the record. This enables you to analyze where the student is making mistakes. Error analysis enables you to determine if students lack skills in areas such as identifying syllables or phonemes in a word, recognizing initial consonant sounds, or various other error patterns. Observation of an oral reading performance can also determine if the student can differentiate between similarly spelled words and has pronunciation strategies for unfamiliar words. Analysis of these strengths and weaknesses can provide specific direction for working with the student to improve reading performance.

Goodman and Burke (1972) found that a child's omissions, substitutions, additions, and self-corrections in oral reading help teachers assess the extent that the child is monitoring for meaning and attending to spelling and sound-symbol correspondences while reading. Miscues that do not change the meaning of the sentence show that students are using anticipation skills to "make sense" of what they are reading. Miscues that change the meaning tell us that the child is not making solid comprehension links.

Cunningham (1991) suggests that errors that do no change the meaning of the sentence are, in fact, a sign of good reading development. A substitution of the word *can't* for *cannot* indicates that the child is reading ahead and anticipating the words that make sense in the passage. This is the goal of our instruction. When we correct the child for this miscue, it merely teaches the child to slow down and fixate more on the individual words rather than reading for intended meaning. This can cause the child to become a word-by-word reader even when the child transfers this skill to silent reading. When a student makes a miscue that does change the meaning of the sentence, we might stop the child by saying something like, "I missed that part. Can you reread that part to me again?" so the fixation is less on the individual words and more on the concept of making sense of print. If too many interruptions are made, it will discourage children from self-correcting and learning to self-monitor their reading. The power of miscue analysis is that we can see firsthand what readers know and what they do not know. This knowledge then guides the activities that we will select to shape the learning of both the individual and the class.

Phonics as a Foundational Thread

Phonics instruction helps beginning readers understand the relationship between letters and sounds, and letters and words. Phonics is most effective when introduced early in the reading development process. According to *Put Reading First* (Armbuster, Lehr, & Osborn, 2001), "Phonics instruction teaches children the relationships between the letters (graphemes) of written language and the individual sounds (phonemes) of spoken language." This foundational thread helps students understand that there are systematic and predictable relationships between letters, their sounds, and the words they make. A strong grounding in phonics early in the reading process provides students with one more strong foundational thread in the tapestry of effective reading.

⋇ 3 ⋇

Vocabulary

Vocabulary is the meaning and pronunciation of words that we use in communication. It is simply the number of words that we understand or can actively use to listen, speak, read, or write. Each person has four different vocabularies: listening, speaking, reading, and writing. An individual's listening vocabulary is the largest and first to develop, followed by the speaking or oral vocabulary (Snow, Burns, & Griffin, 1998). The reading vocabulary is third to develop followed by our writing vocabulary. For high-volume readers, the reading vocabulary may even become the largest storehouse of word recognition. Each vocabulary set continues to grow and develop with time.

There are two ways to expand our vocabulary sets. We can learn new vocabulary indirectly through everyday experiences or we can have someone directly teach or explain the meaning of a word to us (Armbruster, Lehr, & Osborn, 2001). We learn new words all of our lives indirectly when we hear or see words in different contexts. This learning can take place through listening to conversations, being read to, or by reading new words in context. Word meanings can also be explicitly taught when we are told the meaning of a new word, when we look the word up in a reference source, or when we use other direct methods to find out more about a specific word.

We go through several stages in vocabulary acquisition (Johns & Lenski, 2001). The first stage is when we have no knowledge of a word in any working vocabulary. The second stage is when we've heard the word but are unsure of the meaning. The third stage is having a vague sense of the meaning of the word—we can describe a meaning for the word in general terms. The final stage of vocabulary development is that we understand the meaning fully and can integrate the new word into one or more of our four working vocabularies. As long as the word is activated from time to time through some type of usage, the word will probably remain in our active vocabulary. Words that are not activated or linked to specific episodic memory events may eventually fade from memory if there is no further use of the word or reason to retain it in memory.

How Do We Acquire and Build Vocabulary Knowledge?

Identification of the printed word begins with a visual process that concentrates on the visual forms of the letters that make up the word. After the initial identification of the word is made, it is the context of the sentence that may determine word meaning and even the pronunciation of the word. For example, the word *fall* can either refer to the act of moving from a standing to a prone position on the floor or to a season of the year. The word *read* will be pronounced differently depending on the context of the sentence. Interpreting a word's proper pronunciation while reading is a complex process that must occur within nanoseconds. If the wrong choice is made, the reader will be lost and will need to reread the sentence to regain comprehension.

The English language has one of the largest vocabulary sets of all the languages in the world, containing somewhere around 600,000 to 1,000,000 words (Gillet & Temple, 1990). By the late teen years, speakers of English can claim an average vocabulary of approximately 50,000–60,000 words. In recent years, however, some of this active vocabulary has been shrinking, despite more demanding communication and information processing needs in the global workplace. In 1945, the average American student between the ages of 6 and 14 had a written vocabulary of about 25,000 words. Today, with the advent of television and the Internet, that written vocabulary has dropped to about 10,000 words. It is estimated that students must learn more than 88,000 words by 9th grade to read the textbooks that they are now asked to read (Nagy & Anderson, 1984). It is no wonder that high school students struggle to read their high school textbooks! At a time when the importance of processing information quickly and efficiently continues to grow as information explodes, vocabulary development is an aspect of the reading process that we must take active steps to expand and develop.

Vocabulary knowledge has a direct relationship to background knowledge and high-level comprehension and processing (Nagy & Scott, 2000). The ability to infer or retain new words is strongly dependent on the individual's background knowledge of other words and concepts in the content area. As a result, educators must help students build strong background links to new words and their meanings. As information continues to double exponentially, we must ensure that adults of tomorrow are well prepared to process at high levels and have vast stores of knowledge and full word banks.

Developing and expanding a student's different vocabulary levels is a complex process that requires multiple exposures to words and their meanings (Leung, 1992; Senechal, 1997). As soon as they are ready, students must be taught to use various word-learning strategies as they approach new words in their reading and their classroom environment. It is our job to ensure that vocabulary development is a high priority for every student. By the end of first grade, most children know between 4,000 and 6,000 words (Chall, 1987). Just thirteen words (*a, and, for, he, in, is, it, of, that, the, to, was, you*) account for approximately 25 percent of all words found in school texts (Johns & Lenski, 2001). Only 5,000 words make up 90 percent of the words in elementary school texts (Adams, 1990). Learning vocabulary words has a strong impact on students' comprehension of what they are reading (Nagy & Scott, 2000). High-frequency word lists help students learn to master the most commonly found words in the English language. Students should be taught to read, write, and spell these high-frequency words as soon as possible in their school career. The more words students recognize automatically, the greater their level of reading fluency and comprehension. Researcher

G. Reid Lyon (1998), states, "Some youngsters need to read a word only once to recognize it again with greater speed; others need 20 or more exposures. The average child needs between 4 and 14 exposures to automatize the recognition of a new word." To maximize vocabulary development, effective teachers provide ample opportunities for students to read and hear a large variety of words in their daily environments.

Expanding Student Vocabulary Knowledge

We need to focus on expanding our students' oral and listening vocabularies and then moving words from these vocabularies to students' reading and writing vocabularies. It is vital that we expand the content of the various vocabularies to include new words, their various definitions and usages, and the "shades of meaning" or connotations that are associated with each word. We must then help students align new concepts they are learning to the appropriate terms and vocabulary, thus creating relationship networks. Beck and McKeown (1998) remind us that ideas are tied to other ideas, thus forming a network of relationships in our background knowledge. They state, "When information is encountered in a text, the richer the networks, the more easily the new information can fit into them and thus retained in memory. The relationships also help make the new knowledge useful."

Whenever possible, we should help students build solid links between new words and the student's own background knowledge. Some of the ways that we can encourage vocabulary expansion include the following: extensive reading; directly building background knowledge in students; linking words to other words and experiences; building neural connections in the brain; providing opportunities for playing with words and manipulating words; and providing ways to use words on a daily basis. Beck & McKeown (1998) state that developing vocabulary "requires engaging children in *thinking* about words and applying them to different situations."

Explicit Teaching of Vocabulary

During the reading process, teachers should explicitly teach words that are vital to the comprehension of the material being read so that students can relate these words to the content of the story. An example of a word that might need to be pretaught to students might be the word *dingy* as a synonym for *boat* in a marine story. Many students would not understand this term and would, therefore, miss the content of the story without this vital link. The concept of *boat* would most likely be within the student's background knowledge, so explaining the new term with synonyms the student could understand would be relatively easy.

We should also explicitly teach words that the student is likely to see or encounter again and again in the material being studied. Previewing important terms is particularly important for content-area classes where there are many words that students do not already have in their working vocabularies. This would include scientific or specialized terms, such as *photosynthesis* or *mitosis*, which the student will need in order to comprehend the subject matter being presented. Other words that should be explicitly taught are words that have multiple meanings. An example of this might be the word *bank*, which has several meanings. The student would need to understand that the term could be referring to a financial institution, a curve in the road with a certain slope, or the side of a river, depending on context. Other words that should be directly taught include words that have different pronunciations and different meanings but are spelled the same, such as *bow* as in "a knot with loops for a package" and *bow* as in "the front of a boat." The same goes for words that students often confuse that have the same pronunciation but are spelled differently and have different meanings such as *their*, *there*, and *they're*. Some additional ideas for explicitly teaching new vocabulary to students can be found in the suggestions which follow.

Word Play

Find multiple ways to help students "play" with words using acrostics, Hink Pinks, Wordles, puns, palindromes, and other such word play games in all grades. Any teacher supply store has racks of these types of books available for purchase. Include new ways for students to learn about words and their meanings to keep the pace lively and fun.

Definition Game

Place sight words or subject matter vocabulary words on three-by-five-inch cards. Have students take turns drawing a card from a deck placed face down. When they draw words, students must say the word and use it correctly in a sentence or give a definition. If the student is correct, he or she takes the card and places it in his or her stack. The student with the most cards at the end of play is the winner. The other students can challenge anyone's definition or sentence by using the dictionary to disprove the definition or sentence usage. The teacher is the final judge in the event of a team dispute that is unresolved.

I'm Thinking of a Word

In this game, the selected person looks around the room at words posted on the wall or on word walls and then says, for example, "I am thinking of a word that begins with 'b' and has two syllables." Students then guess the word that the person has in mind. A harder version is to have students think of a word, write it on a small chalkboard, then allow other students to guess the word based on the clues that the students give about their word. Students can continue to give extra "clues" about the word until the correct word is guessed. A variation of the "I'm thinking of a word" game is a type of "Hangman" game. Draw the spaces to represent the letters of the word. Instead of random guesses, give students clues about the word in question such as "My word has two syllables." Limit the game to words present in the environment or expand it to all words the students have in their word knowledge base for a harder version of the game.

Palindromes

Explain to students that a palindrome is a word that is the same spelled forward as well as backward. Examples of palindromes are the words *mom* and *dad*. Ask students to find words that are palindromes. While much more difficult, students can even find or invent sentences that would qualify as palindromes.

Bluff

A fun game to help students learn new vocabulary is called Bluff. In this game, students are divided into teams of four and are each given one word. The students must look up the dictionary definition of the word and write it on one of the cards. One student takes the real definition card. The students then work together to come up with three false definitions for the word that could seem plausible. Student groups take turns presenting their definitions to the rest of the class. Students in the other teams must guess who has the real definition card and which students are bluffing. Points are awarded to the team that identifies the correct definition.

Riddles

Write a series of vocabulary words on the board. Create a riddle for each word. As clues are given, students try to guess which vocabulary word meets the clues given in the riddle.

Rewriting Paragraphs

Find a news or magazine article (or create one) that either has a lot of fancy words or a lot of simple, short words. Have students go through the story and either clip the article by changing the long words to shorter, space-efficient words or by changing the short, abbreviated words to longer and more descriptive words. The change should not essentially change the meaning of the original article. Teams should read their changes to the class for the whole class to enjoy. Extra recognition can be given to teams who use creative but appropriate substitutions in their renditions.

Class Thesaurus and Dictionary

Develop a class thesaurus in big book size. As new words and synonyms are learned during the school year, add them to the class thesaurus.

Students can refer to the book during writing and reading activities. Students in content-area classrooms can make special unique dictionaries such as the "Biology Dictionary" or the "Chemistry Dictionary" in big book size as a way to record new terminology they are learning in an easy and fun way.

Password

Create a "Password" game for students just like the old TV game show. Selected words are hidden in a paper folder and given to one individual on each team. The remaining members on the team are then asked to guess the word based on oral one-word clues the password holder provides about the word. Points are given for correctly identified words.

Building Vocabulary Fluency

To enhance vocabulary fluency, ask groups of students to write as many words as they can think of that fit a specific category within a specified time limit. Categories can be broad, such as transportation, sports, animals, words around the home or around the school, items found in a kitchen, or green items. Groups can compare their words and see which group can come up with the most words. Extra points can be given for words on each list that no one else has written. These games build thinking fluency skills as well as vocabulary.

Daily Mystery Word

Entice students with a daily mystery word. Write a special vocabulary word and its definition on a card and then provide students with a series of clues to help them guess the identity of the mystery word of the day. The cards can be collected, shuffled, and then used as "vocabulary trivia," where students have to give either the definition of the word or identify the word being defined as the clue is given.

Word Flag

While using the overhead with a reading passage, you can literally lift words off of the page to highlight a special word for students. Glue a horizontal strip of tag board to a tongue depressor stick to make a flag. When a word that you want to highlight is found, place the word flag in the air in front of the projection beam. You can "catch" the word on the word flag to show to students. Students will really enjoy seeing words being lifted off the page in this fun way (Cunningham, 2000).

Featured Words

Provide students with 10 new vocabulary words per week on a bulletin board or chalkboard. Introduce all the words on the first day and then focus on two words per day with the students. Have students explore ways to use the word correctly. During the week, listen to student conversations and point it out when the student uses one of the weekly featured words in normal conversation. Special points or prizes can be awarded to students or student teams for each occasion that they are "caught" using a featured word correctly.

Playing with Prefixes

The prefixes *dis, in, im, ir, il, re,* and *un* account for over 58 percent of all prefixed words. Ask students to work in teams to make a list of all of the words that begin with these letters. Ask students to divide the list into words that have a prefix and words that simply start with the given letters. Ask students to discuss how the prefix helps identify the meaning of the prefixed word.

Pronunciation Guides

Many students do not know how to use the pronunciation guides in dictionaries. Be sure to teach not only the use of guidewords and how to locate words in the dictionary, but also how to use the pronunciation symbols to pronounce the word once it is found. Practice by reading difficult sentences written in pronunciation symbols. The students will enjoy the laughs and will learn a very valuable skill.

Special Dictionaries

Creating dictionaries for nonhumans is a fun way to get students to think about vocabulary specific to a topic or group. Ask students to suppose that other creatures or things made dictionaries of the words important to them. What would a dictionary for a specific animal look like, or one for plants or computers?

Onomatopoeia

Teach students the concept of onomatopoeia (pronounced "on o mah ta pee ah") by asking students to look for words we use in everyday language that imitate real sounds. An example is the word "sizzle" to describe something frying in a pan of hot oil. Have students illustrate the words they find that fit the onomatopoeia label. Have students read stories or poems that are loaded with onomatopoetic words.

Concentration Bulletin Board

Develop a "concentration" bulletin board that has a vocabulary word and the meaning hidden behind 36 or so hidden squares in a six-by-six-inch grid. Students strive to make matches by uncovering two numbered squares at a time. If a match occurs, the student gets two points. If no match occurs, another student gets to attempt to make a match.

Word Play

Get small, blank wall tiles from a tile or hardware store to equal approximately 100 per student. Using a permanent marker, make three to four copies of consonants and five to six copies of vowel letters on the tiles by placing one letter per tile. Put the tiles in a large resealable bag for each student for easy and fast distribution. Ask students to change one word into another word by laying out the starting word in their tiles and then manipulating them as directions are given. Give step-by-step directions to change the word from one word into the target word. Example: Start with the word "mat." Change the *m* to *b*. What word does it make? Change the *a* to *i*. What word does it make? etc. This activity is good for vocabulary development with word wall words as well as for enhancing decoding skills.

Note: Sometimes a tile store will save odd lots or leftover tiles from a job for you and you can get them for free. Be sure to tell them that you need light-colored tiles only for this purpose.

"ABC" Books

Read a couple of "ABC" picture books to students. Have students write an "ABC" story to encourage fun with language. Give the books to lower-grade classrooms. A more advanced version of this activity requires a great deal of additional higher-level thinking. Using a retelling of a favorite fairy tale or nursery rhyme, students rewrite the story by starting the first sentence with a word that begins with the letter "a." The second sentence must start with a word that begins with the letter "b," while the third sentence must start with a word that begins with the letter "c," and so on. If the stories are typed, students can have fun creating a more interesting font for the beginning letters so the alphabet portion of the sentence stands out. The stories can also be placed sentence by sentence on 26 pages and illustrated in a book format.

Alliterative Sentences

Students can have a good time working with a team to develop alliterative sentences from "a" to "z." For example, students might write, "All alligators are allowed apples." Creative thinking on constructing sentences continues "a" to "z." Dictionary use is encouraged on this one.

Making New Vocabulary Stick

Researchers Robbins and Ehri (1994) studied the most effective methods of vocabulary development. Their conclusions were that vocabulary instruction methods where students are given both the definition of the word as well as examples of usage and practice with usage have produced the largest gains in both vocabulary as well as comprehension skills. Several studies have verified that semantic webs, word maps, and graphic organizers where students can graphically show relationships provide a memory link that is an effective vocabulary-building technique

(Anders, Bos, & Filip, 1984; Heimlich & Pittelman, 1986; Johnson, Toms-Bronowski, & Pittelman, 1982). It is important to note, however, that merely creating these maps without discussion around the vocabulary term is not effective (Stahl & Vancil, 1986). Students must discuss and work with the words for these techniques to produce lasting vocabulary gains. The following techniques will help will long-term retention of vocabulary.

Etymology

Introduce the field of etymology to students. Ask students to research the origin or history of various words. Teach students the meanings of prefixes, root words, and suffixes. Give students some sample words and ask students to figure out the meanings by using their "word detective" skills prior to checking the actual meaning in the dictionary. Compare how close their prediction came to the actual definition. This will help students learn to analyze a new word by features when they encounter one while reading.

Word Origins

Have students explore English words that have foreign origins. Students can make lists classifying words by their country of origin. Compare and contrast how close the American English meaning is to the meaning of the word in the original language of the word. Students will also be surprised at how many English words have been borrowed from other languages.

Picture Journals

Ask students to keep word picture journals of new words they encounter. Students create the journal by leaving several blank pages in their journal for each letter. When a new word is discovered, students enter the word into the proper section and create an illustration that helps them remember and understand the meaning of the word. Students can enter the definition in their own words or use the definition from a dictionary. Students should be encouraged to use their picture journal as a resource whenever they write or are reading new material.

Idioms and Figurative Language

As students are learning idioms or figurative language, ask them to draw comparisons between literal and figurative meanings. Students, particularly non-English speaking students, will enjoy adding these colorful words and phrases to their vocabulary and sharing their humorous pictures with others in their class on the literal and figurative meanings of these words and phrases. Two excellent books for teaching idioms to students are P. Parish's *Amelia Bedelia* (1963) and M. Terban's *Mad as a Wet Hen* (1987).

Word Map

When students learn a new word, ask them to make a graphic organizer, semantic map, or concept map to explain the new word and its relationship to meaning or other content. The map can contain such categories as "What is the definition?" "What are some examples or non-examples of this?" "What are the characteristics of the word?" "What are other categories that belong to this word?" and so forth. Students can then make a picture map of the new vocabulary term. This will give them a much greater understanding of the new vocabulary word. This strategy is useful from 1st grade through high school.

Show and Tell

Involve students in a word "show and tell" on a frequent basis. Students can draw pictures, find pictures, or bring in relevant items to instruct their peers in important vocabulary concepts or new terms they have learned.

Categories

Give students a list of 20–25 words. Ask them to analyze the words and to then categorize the words in any logical way that they can describe for others. Students may use any type of graphic organizer or organizational format that fits the words and their categories. Ask students to discuss their organizational patterns with the class.

Illustrations

Ask students to think about words or phrases that can be illustrated artistically to show their meaning. Have students illustrate various words such as *tall, short, thick* and so forth so that the artistic rendition clearly shows the meaning of the word or phrase. For example, *tall* can be written in tall, skinny letters to show the concept while *fat* can be written in thick, chunky letters. Asking students to illustrate a word entirely with pictures can take this word illustration concept further. An example would be a picture of a tooth next to a picture of a brush to illustrate the word *toothbrush.*

Colorful Phrases

Have students think of and list colorful phrases they hear or find in reading that are related to animals. Examples include "Don't make a pig out of yourself," or "I don't give a hoot." A higher-level adaptation can be to write an entire story using the list of phrases the students develop.

Using Context Clues for Word Meaning

Students need to understand the use of context clues and how to use dictionaries and other reference materials to research the contextual meaning of a word. They need to understand how to apply and sort through the various meanings that they find and to use context clues to derive both meaning and proper pronunciation. Understanding the connotations and "shades of meaning" of words is a high-level skill for even native speakers of a language. It is a monumental task for non-English language learners as it involves a high level of processing, background knowledge, and cultural understanding. Helping students explore the depth of meaning in words by examining the multiple meanings connected with each word is helpful for all learners but essential for non-English learners. Older students also need to understand how to use word parts such as affixes, base words, and root words to glean meaning from a word and how to use prior knowledge to interpret the words they encounter.

Another technique that can be taught to older students is to analyze the context to determine if the author provided any clues to the meaning of the word within the text of the passage. There are four common techniques that writers use to provide clues for readers within the context of the message. These techniques can also be taught to students. One method writers use is to provide a definition or an explanation of a new term within the body of the passage to clarify the term for the reader. Another technique is to provide a synonym or an antonym for the new term within the body of the text. In some cases, the author has provided no direct clues but the reader can get a feel for what the meaning of the word might be by reading the whole paragraph. Again, the most effective way of teaching students to actually learn to do this is by hearing us "think aloud" through this process before trying it on their own. Continued class discussions on using these techniques to unlock unknown words will help students develop this concept into a usable strategy. Some strategies that you can use to help students examine context clues include the following activities.

Signal Words

Help students identify "signal words" that may help them identify plausible meanings for a new word. When students guess the correct meanings, have them model thinking aloud for others as they reflect on what clues they used to unlock the probable meaning of the word.

Sticky Notes for New Words

Give students sticky notes and tell them to write new words on the sticky notes and place them in the book at the location of the new words. Students should use the context clues to try to figure out the meaning of the new word as they are reading and should write what they believe might be the meaning of the new word on the sticky note. At the end of the reading session, check the student definitions and help refine any that need further information or further clarification on meaning. Colored "static cling" sheets can also be cut into small strips and placed over words within the text to highlight unknown words. When the students finish reading, they can then enter the words in their student word dictionary along with the definition and the example sentence from the passage where the word appeared.

Context Clues

There are several steps that students should be taught to help decode the meaning of an unknown word via context clues. The first is to consider the word itself. The reader should look for identifiable prefixes, suffixes, or root words in the unidentifiable word. Does any of this interpretation make sense in the context of the sentence? If not, the reader should examine the other words in the sentence and ask what word would make sense in the context of the other words. The reader should then consider the topic of the paragraph and the other words in the paragraph. What might make sense in light of the content of the passage? If all of these strategies fail to produce a viable suggestion of the meaning of the unknown word, then the reader must seek assistance either from another individual or a dictionary. Demonstrate for students with various passages how one strategy might work better than another in each passage.

Thinking Aloud

Model "thinking aloud" strategies as you demonstrate how to identify vocabulary meanings from context clues. Ask students to also "think aloud" as they look for meaning clues in context. Give constructive feedback as needed.

Approaching Unknown Words

Students must develop "word consciousness." This is defined as an awareness of, interest in, and inquisitiveness towards words. Because vocabulary knowledge is a primary link to comprehension, it is essential that we work to expand student vocabulary skills as much as possible in all curricular areas. Use "think aloud" strategies with students to model how to approach unknown words in a sentence. Some strategies that can be taught to students to use when they encounter an unknown word while reading are:

- Using the words in the rest of the sentence to predict a word that would make sense in the sentence.
- Sounding out the letters in the word to see if the word is a recognizable word.
- Looking for root words, prefixes, suffixes, or endings that are known in the word.
- Trying to pronounce the word to see if the word is a recognizable word.
- Continuing to read the passage to see if the meaning becomes clear with additional reading.
- Using a dictionary, asking someone for help, or skipping the word.

Good readers keep trying strategies until they find one that works for them and helps them to understand what they are reading. Poor readers, on the other hand, often simply skip the words they don't readily know, thus losing key meanings from the passage. Failure to maintain comprehension soon has struggling readers giving up on the text altogether.

Word Walls and Their Use in the Classroom

A word wall is a classroom bulletin board posted with words that are important for the students to learn. Classrooms of all grade levels and subject areas should have word walls featuring language that students need in their developmental stage or that is unique to the discipline. Word walls begin as blanks and fill up as words are introduced and worked with in the classroom. It is not enough to simply have a word wall in the classroom. To develop solid vocabulary concepts and background knowledge, the students must work extensively with the words that are introduced on the word wall (Cunningham, 2000). As we have discussed previously, learning words requires many exposures over time for the word and its associated meaning to become easily accessible in the student vocabulary knowledge base.

Teachers can work with words on the word wall by featuring words with rhyme patterns, examining phonemic similarities and differences, or looking at specific features of the words. For example, we might help the students look at adding endings to the words to see how they are changed. Some typical endings that might be introduced are: *y, ly, er, est, ed, ing, s,* and other changes like doubling a letter and changing the *y* to *i*. Word wall work should probably be limited to 10 to 15 minutes per day. Depending on the age of the child, five to seven words should be introduced per week. At this pace, the students would be exposed to approximately 175 to 250 different words during the school year.

Reading expert Patricia Cunningham (2000) advises that for younger children, words should be clapped out, chanted by letters or sounds, and then written so that multiple modalities can be linked to the learning. Pink colored boxes can also be drawn around the individual words, outlining the height of the letters in the word. This will help students identify the word by shape as well as by letter combination. For upper grade students in content-area classrooms, a word wall might consist of word families that end with similar endings, such as *biology, zoology,* and *graphology*. Prefixes and suffixes and their related meanings are helpful to unlocking new vocabulary terms. Brown and Cazden (1965) indicate that approximately 30 root words, prefixes, and suffixes provide the basis for more than 14,000 commonly used words in the English language. Those words are: *ab* (away from); *ad* (to, toward); *co, con, com, col, cor* (together, with); *de* (away, down, out of); *dis* (not, opposite); *ex* (out of, formerly); *in, im, il, ir* (in, not); *pre* (before); *pro* (forward); *re* (back, again); *un* (not, opposite); *able* (capable of, worthy of); *ance, ence, ancy, ency* (act or fact of doing, state, quality); *er, or* (person or thing connected with, agent); *ful* (full of, abounding in); *less* (without, free from); *ly* (like, characteristic of); *ment* (state of, quality of); *tion, sion, xion* (action, state result); *phon* (sound, speech); *tele* (distance); *meter* (measure); *cap* (to sieze, take or contain); *audio* (to hear); *vid, vis* (to see or look at); *spect* (to observe, watch); *inter* (between); *sub* (under); *mis* (wrong); *trans* (across or beyond); and Latin verbs *tenere* (to have, hold) as in *tenable, tenacious, tenant; mittere* (to send, launch) as in *message, missile* and *missive; facere* (to do, make) as in *faction, artifact, manufacture;* and *scribere* (to write) as in *scribble, scribe* or *script*. Learning these key word parts will help students unlock many words found in their day-to-day reading. Rhyme patterns are another feature that should be emphasized with students because this is the technique that adults most often use to identify new words while reading.

During the primary years, mark words on the word wall that have rhyme patterns that would help with the spelling of other words (Cunningham, 1991). Some of the words that could be emphasized are: *at, look, went, not, am, and, can, will,* and *make*. During word practice, students could be given sentences as a "dictation" with variations of words from this group to practice spelling. For example, say, "Mary sent the book to Bill." Students are directed to use the pattern words on the word wall to form the needed spelling changes for the word practice and sentence dictation. This gets them in the habit of thinking of words that have similar construction. Older disabled readers can also benefit from learning the relationship of pattern spelling to their own reading and writing as well. Very young students might also be asked to just list other words that rhyme with a particular pattern word such as: "Write three words that rhyme with *look*."

Make individual word walls unique to students by putting words in a file folder that the student has at his or her desk. The mini-word walls can also be used as "privacy shields" in the classroom during writing activities. This can also be helpful for elementary classrooms where wall space is limited. Older students can keep their words in a notebook or "word log" so that they can refer to them as needed.

For older students, word walls can contain content-area words as well as prefixes, suffixes, and root words. For example, in a science class, content-area words that emphasize "ology" words could be featured to help students link their learning to concepts they already know. By repeating the graphic representation of these components, students will be better prepared to decipher words they encounter in their classrooms and textbooks. Try the following ideas to enhance your classroom word walls.

New Words

Have students collect new words from reading, conversations that they hear, and from their environment. Place all of these words on a special bulletin board. Ask each contributor to write his or her word, the definition, and a telling example of how it might be used in a sentence. Also ask students to draw or illustrate the meaning of the word. As each word is added to the bulletin board, ask students to also add the information in their own personal classroom dictionaries.

Categorizing Names

Ask students to categorize their last names as to what they represent. Some typical categories might be places, people, things, animals, adjectives, and jobs. Students might be sent to collect and categorize additional names as a homework assignment.

Dead Words

Ask students to develop bulletin board lists of "dead," "tired," or "outlawed" words for trite, overused words frequently present in their writing. Students will have fun developing the appropriate background motif for the bulletin board for the label chosen. One idea is to use the concept of "Rest in Peace" for tired, overworked words students use in their writing. Ask students to work together to make lists of other, more interesting words that can replace overworked words. Ask students to "juice up" their writing by omitting the "dead" words from their writing. Have students point out how authors choose interesting and unusual words to make their writing more lively.

Language Collectors

Have students become "language collectors" by asking them to find examples of alliteration, onomatopoeia, figures of speech, or idioms from the newspaper headlines. Construct a special bulletin board for students to display and highlight their finds. Change the bulletin board to feature a new topic each month.

Vocabulary Is a Key to Successful Reading Performance

Teaching vocabulary is a complex process that demands multiple strategies and many opportunities to interact with new vocabulary terms. Broadening the experiences that students have in the classroom and the amount of times that new words are highlighted will have a solid impact on the expansion of all four student vocabularies. As the world of knowledge explodes, we must ensure that our students are prepared to meet the challenges of sifting through mountains of data and information in a responsible and effective way. Fostering a love of playing with words in the classroom can help us to ensure that the vocabulary thread is well woven throughout the reading tapestry.

✦ 4 ✦

Fluency

Fluency is the ability to read a text accurately, smoothly, quickly, and with expression. There are two types of fluency—oral fluency and silent reading fluency. Silent reading tends to be a better method of assessing reading comprehension, while oral reading provides important information about the reader's proficiency in applying reading strategies (Johns & Lenski, 2001). Fluency develops over time with practice.

A fluent reader reads effortlessly, uses expression, and can read and recognize words quickly. Students who read fluently have developed automaticity (Samuels, 1994) and understand how to group words quickly to gain meaning from the text. When students possess automaticity, they do not have to attend to the task of decoding and can focus their energies on comprehension. Fluent readers use decoding skills to move quickly through the material to achieve comprehension. Fluent readers have a good knowledge of vocabulary and good word identification skills. In addition, fluent readers can make connections between the text and their own background knowledge (Armbruster, Lehr, & Osborn, 2001).

Some students are able to read orally with speed, expression, and smooth decoding but they do not understand what they read. These students are not yet fluent readers because fluency also requires comprehension. To be termed a "fluent reader" with a particular text, an individual must be able to demonstrate both proper decoding as well as comprehension of the text. Fluent readers are able to concentrate on making meaning from what they are reading, because they don't need to struggle with decoding. The stronger the reader's fluency in reading a specific passage, the greater the resulting comprehension with the material being read.

Fluency is not a stage of development. Fluency changes depending on the reader's understanding of the vocabulary, his or her background knowledge and familiarity with the content being read, the purpose of reading, and the type of text being read. Word recognition alone does not translate into increased fluency or comprehension. It is important to provide students with practice with various types of texts to build fluency with many types of text.

How and Why Does Fluency Change?

A reader's level of fluency changes with the level of difficulty of the material and the reader's level of background knowledge in the content that the text is about. We read *about* something and it is this background content knowledge that makes a difference in how well we understand the material. Individuals who possess extensive knowledge on a topic prior to reading are able to recall more of the important information from a text than can individuals with a lower level of initial knowledge in the topic (Beck & McKeown, 1998). In 1979, researchers Spilich, Vesonder, Chiesi, and Voss and studied this link by analyzing the comprehension of adults with a high and a low initial knowledge of baseball. Subjects read a passage about a baseball game and were then asked to recall the text that they had read. Individuals from the "high-knowledge" group recalled more of the information and, in addition, there were significant differences in the quality of what they remembered. High-knowledge readers were more likely to remember information of greater significance to the game of baseball while low-knowledge readers were more likely to remember less significant details from the passage such as the weather. Pearson, Hansen, and Gordon (1979) reinforced this observation in a similar study with two groups of 2nd grade students whose main differing variable was their background knowledge of spiders. When asked implicit and explicit questions regarding information in the passage, the high-knowledge children were better able to answer implicit questions based on the text. From this research, we know that readers with higher levels of background knowledge in a subject comprehend more of the text and process the text at higher levels than do low-knowledge readers. This reinforces the importance of making sure that students have adequate background before asking them to learn new material from a text.

Background knowledge and prior experience are necessary to allow reading fluency to result in comprehension. Students must be practicing the skill of fluency on material that is not beyond their reading and comprehension ability. There is much research to document the benefits of extensive reading practice and the improvement of reading fluency when students read more at their independent reading level (National Institute of Child Health and Human Development, 2000).

We can test the relationship between background knowledge and fluency for ourselves. Take a look at the following list of words. Determine if there are any words that you do not recognize in the list below. As an adult reader, you are probably able to read and pronounce each word listed and quite possibly even able to give a short definition of the word or use it in another sentence.

WHEN	INEQUALITY	TERMS
CONTAINS	HAVE	VARIABLE
FACTOR	SIDES	BOTH
FORM	EQUIVALENT	DO
NOT	WITH	SIDE
THIS	BE	AS
OTHER	ADDING	ADDITIVE
INVERSE	NEGATIVE	OF

Because the words are common words that are in the vocabulary of most adult readers, most individuals would probably be confident that they could explain a passage containing these words to another person. You would probably say that you would have no problem understanding any of these words in written form and that your fluency and decoding would be high. You would probably conclude that you recognize these words at a level of automaticity. It is likely that all of the words listed above would be in your reading vocabulary. Now, read the following paragraph and see if you still say that you have a level of automaticity and comprehension with the reading passage.

> When the inequality contains terms that have the variable as a factor and terms that do not have the variable as a factor on both sides, form an equivalent inequality that has all the terms with the variable as a factor on one side and the terms not having the variable on the other side. This can be accomplished by adding the additive inverses (negatives) of the terms to both sides of the inequality. (Gobran, 1978)

Unless you are teaching math or have recently taken a college algebra course, you probably do not have the background knowledge necessary to understand and be able to explain the passage to another person easily and fluently. In fact, some of you may even be having flashbacks to your math phobic days right about now! As we can see from this example, background and prior learning for all readers is essential to make sense of material we read. Fluency and comprehension are highly dependent on having the background necessary to make sense of the message.

As we have seen, not having extensive background knowledge is a severely limiting factor when it comes to learning. This is especially true of students from high-poverty homes who do not have high exposure to extensive background knowledge and who do not use formal speech patterns in their everyday lives. While not impossible, it is very difficult for these students to become fluent readers until they have a strong foundation of background knowledge, formal English patterns, and experience as a foundation for building new knowledge. This is also true for English language learners in the classroom, some of whom have a different cultural background that they bring to the learning experience. Expanding the background knowledge and oral language skills of these children early in their lives is critical. According to G. Reid Lyon, research psychologist and chief of the Child Development and Behavior Branch of the National Institute of Child Health and Human Development at the National Institutes of Health, early intervention and support is crucial for at risk students:

> We have learned that for 90 percent to 95 percent of poor readers, prevention and early intervention programs that combine instruction in phoneme awareness, phonics, fluency development, and reading comprehension strategies and are provided by well-trained teachers can increase reading skills to average reading levels. However, we have also learned that if we delay intervention until nine years of age (the time when most children with reading difficulties receive services), approximately 75% of the children will continue to have difficulties learning to read throughout high school. (1998)

What Can We Do to Increase Fluency in Readers?

Students must hear fluent readers model reading and must be given time to improve their delivery with strong adult coaching. Adults, both at home and at school, should model smooth, expression-filled reading for students. We can call this "reading with oomph!" Students need to hear how a fluent reader sounds and how he or she uses expression and phraseology to help make meaning out of the words. Students, especially those with limited oral backgrounds, must make the connection that reading is just "talk written down." Until this connection is made in student's minds, they will have difficulty making the connection between talk that they hear every day and the letters and words they see on a piece of paper. If students do not have fluent readers to listen to, read with, and model in the home, it is even more essential that good adult and student models work with the child to model and coach fluency skills at school. It is difficult to monitor meaning when you are still stumbling over the words in an effort to decode them.

To increase word recognition and fluency skills, have students read as much material at their independent reading level as possible. Students should be reading material they can read with at least a 95 percent accuracy rate (Allington, 2001). A quick and easy way to determine whether students are reading material at the appropriate level of difficulty is to have students read several sentences or paragraphs in a couple of minutes. If the student makes five or more reading mistakes in the material during the short reading period, the material is too difficult and he or she should select a less challenging material to read independently. For older students, if the student makes more than 7 miscues per 100 words, the material is too difficult. Fluency is gained when students practice material that is adequately challenging for them but not too challenging. A lack of fluency can signal inadequate sight vocabulary or lack of word identification skills, particularly in an older reader. We must drop back the level of the material until we reach a level comfortable for the student. High interest, low vocabulary materials are often available to ensure that students can practice with material with which they have some level of background knowledge and interest.

Asking students to deliberately practice increasing their speed and accuracy will increase their awareness of reading fluency. An easy test to determine a student's reading rate is to take a timed sample of a student's reading performance at his or her independent level of reading (Hasbrouck & Tindal, 1992). The reading rate (number of words in the passage divided by time needed to read the passage) on similar material taken over time can show growth in the student's ability to process text at increasingly more efficient speeds. For a 1st grade student, we might expect a reading speed of 40–60 words per minute by the end of the school year. Although rates will vary by student and with the material being read, a 4th grade student might be reading around 114–120 words per minute while an 8th grade student might be expected to read between 150–180 words per minute.

To build strong fluency skills, a strategy called "guided reading" has been effective with all types of students (Fountas & Pinnell, 1996). In this instructional technique, the model reader (teacher, parent, or peer) reads the selection, modeling fluent and thoughtful reading. The student then rereads the passage on his or her own, practicing and rehearsing for fluency. Rereading and practicing the text four or five times is usually sufficient for most students. After the rehearsal period, the student reads the passage back to the "coach," who offers feedback and encouragement. The student should be reading short passages or stories, poems, plays or specific paragraphs that are appropriate for his or her development, background, and independent reading level. Repeating a passage over and over again can give the reader confidence, speed, and a solid understanding of the meaning of what is being read. Having the coach to listen to the student allows for immediate guidance and feedback to improve the performance. Feedback that is direct and immediate helps the student improve and perfect the delivery and fluency level of the material.

Reading Practice Enhances Fluency

According to the research of Eldredge, Reutzel, and Hollingsworth (1996), "round-robin" reading, when compared to a "shared book" experience, has not been shown to be effective at improving student fluency or comprehension. This is because in a round-robin reading situation, the student generally only reads a small portion of text at any one time. In addition, the student reads the text only once and there is little opportunity for the student to increase or improve his or her skills through extensive practice or performance feedback. Other limitations of round-robin reading are that there is no additional time for rehearsal or improvement with the given material. We often simply move on to the next reader in the sequence, so the material is never reread or more fully explored.

In the shared book approach (Cunningham & Allington, 1999), the same book is read and reread orally multiple times. For primary classrooms, the teacher often reads the story to the class during the first reading. During subsequent readings, the children often join in on parts of the reading, particularly when the book contains a predictable pattern or a strong sense of rhythm. During the readings, the teacher may stop periodically to ask or answer questions or discuss key elements of the text or images in the book. Thus the name "shared" readings. In the study by Eldredge, Reutzel, and Hollingsworth (1996), students in the shared book instructional approach outperformed their "round-robin" comparison group in vocabulary, word analysis, word recognition, fluency, and text comprehension abilities. A form of "shared reading" can be done at upper grades by having students read a segment of text and then asking them to summarize the text. Some additional ideas that you can use to enhance student fluency are:

Books with Conversation

Because young students or struggling readers need to understand that reading is "talk written down," we can help them make this association by using big books that have conversation in them. Select books with extensive conversational text for shared reading time. Practice reading the conversational parts orally with students so they develop a strong association between the two ideas. An example of a book that might be used for primary students for this purpose is *5 Little Monkeys Jumping on the Bed* by Eileen Christelow (1990). Poems with conversation or short plays work well for older students.

Radio Plays

Students can make the same link with plays that are performed for an audience or recorded as "radio plays." Ask students to pay attention to the rise and fall of a reader's voice and the word phrase and grouping strategies that the reader uses. Demonstrate the rise and fall flow of the sentences with your hand as the material is read. Have students also use their hands to signal the rise and fall of the material as the adult reads or a partner reads. This strategy increases a student's awareness of the lilt and flow of the language. Have students practice the material until they can deliver it with the proper level of fluency and expression.

Trying Different Voices

Put a sentence on the board or overhead. Ask students to read the sentence with different voices or from the perspective of different characters. Some examples of characters to try are a kindly grandma, a policeman, an angry mother, a teacher, a little child, and a stern father. Extend this idea by helping students dramatize a scene or book written with a specific dialect. Students could even "translate" a specific passage into a different voice or dialect entirely, such as Juliet as a "Valley girl" or a speech by Macbeth as a '30s gangster. Younger children can rewrite fairy tale scenes from the perspective of another character such as the wolf in *Little Red Riding Hood* or the wicked witch in *The Wizard of Oz*.

Phrasing

For a beginning reader, place slash (/) marks in the paragraph after sets of words and ask students to try to read each word group as a complete set before stopping. This strategy can help a "choppy" reader learn to consider a group of words as one reading bite.

Playing with Punctuation

Show students groups of sentences or paragraphs that can be punctuated differently depending on meaning. A sample sentence of this type is "Mary Louise my daughter is late." Ask students to read the sentences using punctuation in different places to see how it changes the meaning from "Mary, Louise, my daughter, is late" to "Mary Louise, my daughter is late." Place slash marks between words or groups of words and have students read the sentences with the pauses as indicated. Move the slash marks and reread the sentences. How does the inflection of the sentence indicate a different meaning? This will help students see that punctuation can impact meaning. Give students some examples to punctuate in different ways. Ask students to explain the nuances or differences in meaning that they observe in each example.

Choral Reading

Have students read chorally along with a fluent reader as the fluent reader points to the material being read on a chart or in a big book. This is a particularly effective technique where the material is patterned or predictable. The material should be read often enough that children know the material and can easily join in the reading. Occasionally the reader should stop and allow the children to fill in the next word or phrase when a predictable point is reached in the story.

Dictation

Have students dictate a paragraph or short story of their own creation to another person. The writing is typed up and given back to the student to practice reading. When they have sufficiently practiced the passage and can read it fluently, the students present the passage to the teacher or to another important adult. The ownership of reading what they wrote themselves is a powerful motivator for students struggling to improve their reading. Students can later add to this story or create other stories that they can practice reading. A book of "My Own Writings" can even be assembled so the students have a collection of their writing. The students should be encouraged to reread the passages to improve performance and delivery.

Rehearsal Reading

Ask students to "echo" read a story with you one time through. (Echo reading is when one individual reads and is echoed by other readers immediately afterward.) For the second reading, parts are assigned to different groups. Parts are rotated until each group has read all of the parts. Students then read the parts in small groups of four or five students. The material is then well rehearsed and can be sent home for students to practice with their parents. This technique is good for short books, stories, chants, rhymes, or poems.

Reading Pairs

To read fluently, students have to practice reading. This means that they have to read themselves, not listen to other children, who are also learning to read, practice their own skills. Instead of having students read round-robin style, pair students and have them actively read with a partner during the reading time. Pairings may be made between readers of the same ability or between a more able and less able reader. Pairings should be made high-average, average-average, or average-low. Pairings between the highest and the lowest readers should be avoided. Readers coach one another and provide assistance to their partners as needed. Have the pairs be prepared to present the material to you or another adult when they feel confident that they can deliver the material easily and comfortably.

Playing Characters

Find a play or a book that has many characters and a lot of dialogue. As characters are introduced in the story, assign a student to each character. When the story is read the second time, have each student read the lines for the character they have been assigned. Practice reading the material with feedback given on the student's expression until the students can move easily through the material with appropriate expression and smooth fluency. The material can be tape recorded as a radio play, acted out for an audience, or recorded on videotape.

Increasing Reading Rates

Locate simple passages of one to four paragraphs in length for students to read at their independent level. Encourage students to increase their speed while still maintaining good comprehension. Time the students' reading by calculating the number of words in the passage divided by the time needed to read the passage and record this number. At the end of the reading, ask students to list the 5 W's about the passage they have read. If the student can list the information accurately, they can keep the "improved" reading rate. See how fast students can get at reading while still maintaining comprehension. Have students keep a graph to show their rate increases. Help students understand that reading rate is influenced by the level of material they are reading and by what must be done with the text. Teach older readers how to "skim" text rather than reading every word when surface comprehension (such as in reading for fun) is the goal. Slow reading can become a habit if we do not help students learn to vary their reading rate.

Basal Readers

Because basal readers have controlled vocabulary, they should be used to help students develop and improve their fluency. Select stories that the student finds interesting so that reading will continue to be enjoyable for the student. The basal stories can be read and reread with partners in class or with parents at home to improve fluency skills. Set goals with students to improve a specific part of performance such as intonation, speed, or reading with a smooth flow. Basal stories can even be "echo read" or practiced with partners for fluency. Basal reader stories should not be the only reading "diet" of any student but they can be very helpful for developing fluency skills since the vocabulary is more controlled.

Help for Struggling Readers

It is helpful for primary students to point to words with a finger as they read or to use a card beneath their reading to help them keep their place. Untrained eyes do not track well and students must learn to track from left to right to become fluent readers. Fingers or cards help the eyes track more smoothly. Children who have reading problems often have never learned to track from left to right in a smooth flowing pattern from one line to the next. They lose their place frequently and perform many more rereadings of the same material than do fluent readers. Because we want to train beginning readers to look at a small group of words at a time rather than fixating on single words, it is also a good idea to have students use a small index card with a window cut of the appropriate length to accommodate approximately three words. If you choose not to use a "window viewer," a whole "marker" card can simply be placed below the line of print to be read. Students should be taught to move the card forward slowly and smoothly so that they won't lose their place while reading. Older, struggling readers, particularly dyslexic readers, often have difficulty with tracking as well. Three-by-five-inch cards with windows cut out can also help older, struggling readers keep their place. The window card also reminds the student to read "chunks" or groups of words rather than reading word by word. The card (with or without a window) often works better than the finger approach for older students because it seems less immature.

Teachers can have older readers who struggle with reading problems read rhythmic poems or short passages of dialog. Usually, students enjoy reading the dialog from the perspective of different characters in the story or from different emotional viewpoints. Another source of text for older struggling readers is songs, rhymes, or raps. This type of text is interesting to students and not only helps them develop a sense of pattern but also helps them learn to appropriately "chunk" text. The more the students practice on material at their independent level with direct feedback and coaching, the more their fluency will improve. Older students should practice their fluency skills with different types of materials, including fiction and expository, persuasive, and technical reading. High-interest, low-vocabulary books are again recommended. Expose students to many different types of reading such as newspapers, recipes, stories, instruction manuals, and poems so they can get used to reading for a variety of purposes. Encourage children to "listen" to themselves read to assess if what they have read sounded like "real talk." Developing an understanding of the patterns and "lilt" of the English language is especially helpful for non-English learners. The more non-English language learners hear the beat and pattern of the English language, the more quickly they will be able to pick up the language.

After students have rehearsed and are familiar with the pattern of a particular book or poem, an additional strategy for fluency development is a type of cloze technique. In this method, cover or leave out key words in the text. Students read the text and are asked to fill in the missing word as they get to the proper place. Students must anticipate a word that logically "fits" into the selection. The purpose of this activity is to see if the student is able to provide an appropriate word given the context and syntax of the sentence. It does not matter if the word actually is the word that the author used in the selection as long as the word given is an appropriate word for the context.

When students struggle with reading all of the time, we only reinforce in their minds the idea that reading is difficult and that they are not good at it. This leads to resistance and causes the student to continue to fall further behind their age-mates in reading. There is evidence from longitudinal studies that follow poor readers from kindergarten into young adulthood that shows how powerful this link with failure becomes in the struggling reader's mind. Lyon states:

> Poor readers get used to such failure. By the end of first grade, we begin to notice substantial decreases in the children's self-esteem, self-concept, and motivation to learn to read if they have not been able to master reading skills and keep up with their age-mates. As we follow the children through elementary and middle-school grades, these problems are compounded, and, in many cases very bright youngsters are unable to learn the wonders of science, mathematics, literature, and history, because they cannot read the grade-level textbooks. By high school, these children's potential for entering college has decreased to almost nil, with few occupational and vocational choices available to them. (1998)

Students need to experience success with reading to be motivated to continue trying to improve their reading performance. Help students set small reachable goals so that they can see and graph their successes in reading. This will help them see that they can indeed make progress in improving their reading skills.

The more time students of all levels spend successfully reading at their independent reading levels, the more their fluency and reading ability will increase. Good fluency is an underlying thread for weaving the threads of comprehension and the higher-order reading thread. Fluency is a foundational thread that must be woven into the reading tapestry of each student so they can become thoughtful and thorough readers who can identify the ambiguities, nuances, and complexities of text and read with analytic comprehension. Some additional strategies that work particularly well with struggling readers are outlined below.

Reading Along

Ask a struggling reader to select a book, short story, or magazine article that interests him or her. This should be material that the student would like to learn to read. At this point, it does not matter if the material is too difficult for the student as long as the passage is something that she feels motivated to learn to read. A fluent adult reader reads a 5-10 minute segment of the material slowly into a tape recorder (approximately 75-100 words per minute) while modeling good reading fluency. The tape should not have sound effects or music. The student then listens (preferably with a headset) to the material and is asked to follow along with the text as it is being read. After the student listens to the tape for a few times, the student is asked to read along with the adult. When the student feels she or he has a good mastery of the material and can read the material without the assistance of the tape, the student then reads the material to the teacher or other fluent reader for feedback and coaching.

Echo Reading

Students who struggle with reading problems often read "word by word." They do not understand how to "chunk" words and phrases into meaningful groups. As a result, their comprehension is limited. One strategy that teachers can use is called "echo reading." The adult reads a short sentence or phrase alone, modeling good reading fluency. The student is then asked to repeat the same words trying to imitate the adult's patterns and intonation. The adult gives feedback to the student, repeating as necessary, and the rehearsal continues until the student has the proper phrasing, intonation, and flow. This strategy can also be used for an entire class or small group.

Experimenting with Word Groupings

Students need to think about phrasing when they read a passage. To help them practice this skill, type a paragraph, leaving double spaces between each of the words. Ask students to think about the performance of the paragraph and to place slash (/) marks wherever they think the reader should pause. Encourage students to experiment with word groupings to make the most impact in how the passage sounds.

Visualization

Struggling readers often have difficulty visualizing the events or characters in a story while they are reading. Help students visualize the story by making pictures or "movies" in their mind of the story as they read. Ask students to talk about the movies they are seeing and how it helps them see characters and action more clearly. Model your own thinking and visualization process for the students as well.

Identifying Reading Errors

Give the students short paragraphs typed in a double-spaced format. Ask them to make a tape recording of themselves reading the passage. After the first reading, the students (alone or with partners) listen to the reading and place a check mark above all mispronounced words. The students then reread the passage into the tape recorder and record the second reading with check marks in a different color pen on the paper. Students then do this a third or even fourth time. At the end of the practice sessions, the students make a chart or graph to show the number of errors on each reading of the material. Because each rereading should show improvement as the student becomes more familiar with the reading material, this visual should help the students see the progress that they are making.

Fluency and Automaticity Build Solid Readers

Fluent readers read smoothly, accurately, and with good phrasing and expression. Because they do not have to spend so much cognitive energy on simply decoding and identifying the words they are reading, they can devote more time to gathering and interpreting meaning from the text they are reading. Fluent readers can build connections between what they are reading and their own background knowledge and information storehouses. While fluency develops over time and with practice, reader familiarity with similar text and vocabulary terms builds automaticity. A recent large-scale study of reading performance of 4th grade students taking the National Assessment of Educational Progress (NAEP) found that 44 percent of a sample of our nation's 4th grade students scored low in fluency (Campbell, Humbo, & Mazzeo, 1999) . It was also noted that a correlational link between low scores in fluency and low scores in comprehension were also apparent in these students. For this reason, it is essential that the thread of fluency be deliberately focused and strengthened as readers grow and develop.

⚛ 5 ⚛

Comprehension

Comprehension requires making meaning from words when listening, speaking, reading, and writing. Good readers have a purpose for reading and use their experiences and background knowledge to make sense of the text. Making connections is the key to comprehension. We don't comprehend unless we make connections and are able to process the words that we read at the thinking level.

Comprehension is the center of reading. Up to the end of 3rd grade, children are learning to monitor their own level of comprehension while reading. Research is clear that these skills can improve with explicit instruction and training (Elliott-Faust & Pressley, 1986; Miller, 1985; Palincsar & Brown, 1984; Paris, Cross, & Lipson, 1984). Strategies are what we provide to the learner to help him organize and make meaning as he is reading. Marie Clay (1991) states that a strategy is "an operation that allows the learner to use, apply, transform, relate, interpret, reproduce, and reform information for communication."

Reading comprehension is dependent on three factors. The first factor is that the reader has command of the linguistic structures of the text. The second factor is that the reader is able to exercise metacognitive control over the content being read. This means that the reader is able to monitor and reflect on his or her own level of understanding while reading the material. The third and most important criterion influencing comprehension is that the reader has adequate background in the content and vocabulary being presented.

When an effective reader reads for comprehension and understanding, it is an actively engaged and thoughtful process. One of the things that good readers do during the reading process is to make connections between background knowledge and the new information in the text. Readers filter new information against their own background storehouse of information and life experiences and identify and sift relevant from nonrelevant information. Effective readers monitor when the text is not understood or is not making sense and repair faulty comprehension whenever it occurs. Good readers make inferences during and after reading and are adept at synthesizing information within and across texts. In addition to categorizing information, effective readers use prediction and draw conclusions from explicit as well as from implicit information. Effective readers visualize the information in the text as they read and create images using the different senses to better understand what is read (Pearson, Dole, Duffy, & Roehler, 1992; Keene & Zimmermann, 1997).

Literacy Development

As we seek to help students develop their skills in literacy, we need to provide each student with two types of skills. One set of skills allows the reader to understand the mechanics and organization of reading. The other set of skills is more metacognitive in nature and allows students to link their thought patterns to prior information in their brains. Making meaning at both the content and the process level is the key to comprehension. Thinking and meaning-making are at the core of student learning. As Harvey and Goudvis (2000) state, "we must teach our students to access content when they read as well as teach them the strategies they need to better understand text and become more thoughtful readers." When teachers model "thinking aloud" while reading, students can form a better understanding of how to apply the skills and strategies being presented to them.

The goal of teaching various strategies to students is that the students learn to use them automatically as they read. We must carefully model the strategies, provide guidance and coaching to the students, and then allow large blocks of time for students to practice what they are learning. Readers must develop the understanding that reading is an interactive process involving both decoding words and deriving meaning from those words. We have all watched students lose meaning because they are concentrating too much on simply decoding the words. These students have not yet developed the ability to monitor their own comprehension and do not have adequate skills in decoding. As a result, they lose connection with the text and meaning.

Making Sense of Text

As adult readers, we have learned strategies for monitoring our own comprehension and knowing what to do when the material is difficult or our mind has wandered during the reading process. When most successful readers lose comprehension, they stop reading, go back to the start of where meaning was lost, slow down their rate and reread the passage and check for understanding again. If the material is particularly difficult, the reader may even read the material out loud to aid in the comprehension process. Poor readers do not understand that they should take any action when comprehension is lost. Many simply give up since they have no strategies to use to deal with difficult text.

Successful readers have mastered the ability to connect material to their prior knowledge base, make inferences as they read, formulate questions, visualize the information or story action, and synthesize as they read. There are many comprehension skills that we can teach our students. The first is how to monitor their own level of comprehension while reading. Beginning readers can be reminded to "listen" to the words in their heads as they are reading so that they maintain comprehension. More advanced readers can be asked to summarize portions of the text so that they can better synthesize what they are reading. Students also need to know how to reconnect with a text and repair understanding when comprehension is lost while reading. A good way for students to monitor their own comprehension is to make connections while reading. The brain likes patterns and seeks to connect learning to prior knowledge and experiences. Therefore, it makes sense to give the brain more ways to connect the new information with old information. We can teach students how to link what they are reading to their own experiences (text to self), to other texts that they have read (text to text), and to what they know about the world in which they live (text to world). Learning about genres, forms and structures, and author style help readers become aware of literary and stylistic characteristics so they can better relate to the text.

Questioning, Visualizing, and Inferring

Questioning while reading is a key to developing good comprehension. Proficient readers question the content, the author, the events presented, the arguments, and the issues and ideas in the text. Children need to be taught how to ask questions during reading to monitor comprehension as well as to process the information that they are receiving. They must learn to ask, "Does the information make sense?" as they are reading but also, "Does it agree with previously learned information?" Children must learn to determine what judgments they should be making about the new information or author's viewpoint as they are processing the material. Everyone now uses the Internet for finding information, which can be either reliable or unreliable information depending on the source. Because so much research is being done online, training students to ask probing questions is very important.

Proficient readers ask questions before, during, and after the reading process. When we pick up a book in the library or in the bookstore to consider for purchase, we will probably first focus on the title and the author. The book probably caught our eye because of a catchy title, a subject of interest, or because it was written by a favorite author. Next, we will probably search for summative information about the book in the back of the book or on the book jacket. We may then browse through the chapter headings or flip through and read a few pages to see if the material continues to be of interest. We will then make a determination about whether or not the book is something we wish to read. In a bookstore, we may also consider the price of the book as a factor when we make a decision about the book. In a library, we may consider our schedule and the time that may be needed to read the specific book being considered. Many students do not have an understanding of how to even select a book much less ask questions before reading. They need to have adults model this process, otherwise they may be picking the most colorful book or the thinnest book, as students often do when their reading skills are less than they should be for their age.

Visualization is also a key component of good comprehension. Children need to be taught how to "paint a picture in their minds" as they read to visualize characters, settings, and the action of the story. We can help them do this by modeling our own thoughts as well as by asking them to describe or even draw their interpretations of favorite characters or scenes in the story. Visualization helps students better relate to the story, brings life to the story and the characters, and also strengthens imaginative thinking (Harvey & Goudvis, 2000). Older students also need to learn to use photos, diagrams, charts, and maps to help extend and clarify thinking as they read. We can help students organize information by providing them with graphic organizers that help them organize, classify, or sort various forms of information that they are learning.

Other skills that students must develop are the ability to make inferences about what they are reading and the ability to cull important information. Reading expert Susan Hall (1990) tells us, "Inferring allows readers to make their own discoveries without the direct comment of the author." In order to understand the text being read, students must be skilled in reading not only the lines, but between the lines and beyond the lines as well. Being able to separate the important ideas from the extraneous ideas and material is essential to a proficient reader. Students need to understand that purpose for reading is closely linked to what the reader needs to gain from the material. When we read for pleasure, we read differently than we do when we read to answer a specific question or to summarize key information from a textbook. We need to model these skills for students and to explain how the context and purpose determines both pace as well as the level of attention that must be given to the material. Students must also learn to distinguish between essential ideas and important information and to compare and contrast various aspects of the text such as information provided, genres, or author style. They must also understand how to reread text to enhance comprehension and fluency. Some examples of explicit mini-lessons that you might want to emphasize with students include:

- Sense of story (beginning, middle, end, climax, rising action, falling action, dénouement, resolution);
- Distinguishing main idea and supporting details;
- Distinguishing fact from opinion;
- Distinguishing realism from fantasy;
- Summarizing, sequencing, and retelling story events or concept ideas;
- Making inferences and drawing conclusions;
- Determining qualities, motivation, changes in characters and character development;
- Determining purpose for reading;
- Predicting and confirming or refuting predictions;
- Use of figurative language, metaphor and imagery;
- Setting, plot, subplot, theme, conflict/resolution, point of view;
- Antagonist/protagonist, audience, purpose, dialogue, diction;
- Tone, mood, foreshadowing, flashback, irony;
- Making inferences, drawing conclusions, cause/effect; and
- Propaganda techniques, reliability of data, and bias.

Setting the Stage—Preparing Students to Read

Before beginning a reading assignment, we should "set the stage" by linking the student's background knowledge to the new material. For example, we might say, "Last week we read a story about a tiger. Let's list the things that we already know about tigers on our KWL chart (What I know, What I want to know, What I learned) in the first column." We might ask students to then list the information that they still want to know about tigers in the second column. In another lesson, we might say to our students, "Today, we are going to read a story about having to make a difficult decision. Have you ever had to make a really difficult decision in your life? Tell me about a time when that happened to you." Steps like these help the reader relate to the material on a more personal level. Specialized terms and new vocabulary should also be presented so that students have a clear picture of what they will be reading.

To get the most out of the text, we must also prepare students by establishing the purpose for reading in students' minds. As adults, we usually have a purpose for reading even if the purpose is only that we are interested in learning more information about the topic. We should make it clear to students why they will be reading. Is the reading for enjoyment, to answer questions, to complete a graphic organizer, or to generate a summary of the material? This will help students make the connection that the purpose dictates the depth and attention that may be required during the reading process. As teachers, we cannot assume that students understand this critical link between purpose and the intensity of reading that may be required. If the student is reading for enjoyment, the material can be read quickly without much thought to the details presented. On the other hand, if a student will be expected to produce a summary of the material or to take a test over the material, more careful reading including highlighting or note taking would be needed. For example, we might say, "In this short section, please read to identify the actual event that started the Civil War." We might ask students to search for specific things as they read by saying, "As you read this story, look for points where the characters change and place a sticky note in the text with your observations." Graphic organizers of various types can also help students focus their reading in more concrete ways. We can also give students outlines, anticipation guides, and timelines to help them cull the desired information from the text either during or after the reading process.

As you prepare students to read text, you may want to consider having students make predictions about the possible content or important information that might be gleaned from the text. You will want to determine students' prior knowledge with regard to the new information so that you can provide background information as needed and make connections to the reader's personal experiences. You will also need to think about what vocabulary might be needed for good comprehension of the text and how to assist students in learning the needed vocabulary. Assist students in analyzing the material. Take "picture walks" through the book if the book has pictures and make predictions as to content, story progression, or conclusion. If the book does not have pictures, have students examine the cover, chapter titles, and headings, and any summary materials that may be presented such as descriptions on the book jacket, chapter title, chapter summaries, and so forth. Help students get a "feel" for the book or the content contained in the chapter. Assist students in identifying the purpose for their reading. Are students expected to gather information of some type as they read? Will they do something with the data after reading? Will a KWL chart, a graphic organizer, or an anticipation guide help students better prepare for reading? These support items could help students examine their own knowledge of the information before, during, and after reading.

The goal of "before" reading strategies is to build background, make connections between old and new knowledge, introduce new vocabulary, preview or examine the material in detail, make predictions and help readers set a focus for reading. Activities that can help set the stage for reading to take place are include:

Give a Purpose for Reading

When we assign students to read text, students should also always be given a purpose for reading. For example, we can say, "Read to find out why Arthur started his pet business" or "Read to find out how clouds are formed" or "Read to find out the key issues behind the Vietnam War." This helps students ground themselves in the most important aspect of the text. Appoint one student as the leader in the group. The leader helps the group decide how they will approach the material (partners, sharing paragraphs, read silently then discussing, etc.). The group leader is responsible for keeping the group on task and moving through the material via the method of choice.

Classification Activities

Students who have difficulty seeing relationships may also have difficulty drawing conclusions, making inferences, and predicting outcomes. One of the ways that we can help develop this ability in students is by providing students with many opportunities to classify various objects. Classification activities can be simple or complex, but each experience will help students develop the ability to see relationships more readily.

Logical Prediction

Teach students to predict logical words in a sentence by using context clues and sentences with missing words. Write sentences on an overhead and place a flag over one word in each sentence. Ask students to read the sentences and make a guess about what word is hidden behind each flag. Ask students to explain to other students in the class why they think the word they have guessed is a logical guess. Help students understand that the exact word might not always be guessed but that if a word that makes sense is guessed, it is helpful to good comprehension skill building.

Book Selection

Model for students how to select a book for their own enjoyment. Many students do not know how to analyze a book to determine if it is a suitable book for them both in terms of content and readability. Talk to students about what you do when you go into a bookstore or to the library to select a book. What factors draw you to examine, check out, or purchase a book?

Attention to Detail

To help students read nonfiction material with attention to detail, give several sentences to students based on the material. Some of the sentences should be true and some should be false. Before they read the material, ask students to use their background knowledge to predict whether the questions are true or false. After reading the material, ask students to go back over their answers and see if they still believe that their answers are correct based on the new material they have just read. Ask students to identify page and paragraph in the material to support their responses. During discussions about the material, ask students to "prove it" by citing page and paragraph where they found proof to support their viewpoint or answers.

Predictions

As students are reading sections of their textbook, ask them to predict what they might learn in a particular section. Ask them to complete sentence stems such as, "From the title of this section, I predict that this section will tell us…." After reading, match predictions with actual content. How many predictions were accurate?

Activities to Aid Comprehension While Reading

If the work is too difficult and is not at the student's independent reading level, then the student should read with a partner or in a small group and should be given specific directions on what he or she should know or learn as a result of the reading assignment. When material to be read is at a more advanced level than the student's independent reading ability, we might use echo reading (one individual reads and is echoed by the other reader or readers); choral reading (readers read together orally); shared reading (small groups of students share in the reading); partner reading (two individuals read together either silently or orally); or reading in small groups. In most cases, the teacher will want to match or control which students are allowed to work together.

In order to build strong reading skills, students need to engage in as much active practice as possible. Research shows that teachers are more likely to have low-achieving readers read aloud than high-achieving readers (Allington, 1980, 1983; Chinn, Waggoner, Anderson, Schommer, & Wilkinson, 1993; Collins, 1986; Hoffman et al., 1984). Sometimes teachers interpret "active practice" as the need to direct students through the reading process by engaging in round-robin reading practices. As we learned in a prior chapter, round-robin reading is the least effective way to build reading skills. Even high school students can benefit from a paired or small group type of reading practice. A partner group with adequate reading skills might read the material silently and then work together on the post-reading activity. If the students are poor readers, they might choose to find a quiet location and read the pages orally, taking turns reading to one another. In any case, the actual engaged time is much higher and students are more apt to get the task completed in the time allotted.

Another way to help students prepare to read is by helping them to understand the typical patterns that certain types of text follow. Narrative text is a good example of a patterned text that we can teach students to recognize as they are reading. Narrative text typically follows the pattern of establishment of the setting followed by the introduction of the characters. After this, the author usually introduces the problem or conflict followed by background events relating to the problem or conflict. When the story reaches the highest point of dramatic tension or problem, this is identified as the "critical moment" or climax. Following the climax, the author generally provides a resolution to the problem and winds up the action with closure and "falling action." The entire story, when taken together, establishes a central idea or theme. Additional ways to help build students' skills during the reading process include:

Retelling

An easy way to determine if students have good comprehension of the material that they are reading is to ask the student to retell what has been read. If students have good comprehension, they should be able to give a good summary to include all parts of the story, information on key characters, plot summary and action in the story, and how the story ended. The more complex and detailed the retelling, the better the comprehension of the material. Students can retell the story in pictures, with puppets, or by acting out the story or a key scene in the story for high school students. When students read chapter books, they must be able to connect comprehension from chapter to chapter. When discussing the new text material with students, ask students to "recap" the "action to date" in the previous chapters of the book. During "read alouds," stop frequently to ask students to "summarize" the information, action or storyline to date. This helps students maintain continuity and promotes better comprehension of the material.

Recording Story Elements

Give students at least three sticky notes of various colors. Depending on their age and level of sophistication, ask students to find and record several elements of the story such as a major character, a minor character, a turning point, the setting, the title, the author or illustrator's name, the climax, a problem in the story, a solution or resolution in the story, a plot, etc. This activity can be done independently or in a small group depending on the student's level of familiarity with the given elements.

Looking for Specific Information

Give students several sticky notes and ask them to find clues in their reading to answer a specific question. For example, we might ask students to determine what kind of a person the main character is. As the students read, they record information that answers this question on the sticky note, making sure to record where the information was found. When the class finishes reading, students discuss their data and their observations regarding the information they have located. Disagreements are settled by referring to the page and sentence indicated on the sticky note. Sticky notes can also be used to locate interesting or key vocabulary, places where the main characters change during the story, or other key components of the story.

Putting Sentences in Order

Identifying sequence is an important skill for readers as well as for writers. Type up simple passages and then cut the sentences apart. Ask students to work in groups to reassemble the sentences into a logical sequence. Compare the group's rendition to the original work by the author. Discuss with students the information they used to place the sentences into their order and what "signal" words they may have used to determine a logical order.

Identifying the Main Idea

Newspaper articles can help students develop the concepts of main idea and supporting details. Cut out several short articles for students to read. Ask students to quickly read the article and to determine what the passage is "mostly" about. Point out that this is the main idea of the passage. Then have the students write down the details that tell more about the main topic. A good resource to use for this is a "T" chart with the top box holding the topic or main idea and the rest of the "T" holding the details on the topic.

Monitoring Comprehension

Students must be taught to monitor their own comprehension as they read. They should constantly ask themselves, "Does this make sense?" and then be taught to use strategies such as varying the pace or rereading the text when the material no longer is meaningful to them. Teachers should model this behavior aloud as they read to students.

Using Graphic Organizers

Give students a graphic organizer such as a "Character Web," "Main Idea Web," "Story map" or other such organizer. Graphic organizers are visual representations that increase retention and understanding of the material being read. Encourage students to complete the given web with the appropriate relationships as they read the material. Content-area teachers will find this a particularly useful strategy for students to use for nonfiction material to identify key information and relationships within the content-area curriculum.

Keeping a Two-Column Log

Demonstrate to students how to keep a two-column log while they are reading to record their thoughts and feelings about key events in the story. In one column, the student lists key information about the events in the story as they unfold. On the other side of the page, the student lists thoughts, questions, connections, or predictions about what might happen as the story progresses. The student updates this information at key points in the story or as comments arise. For nonfiction material, the student can create one column labeled "important information" and a second column for "why it is important."

Reciprocal Teaching

Reciprocal teaching techniques (Palincsar & Brown, 1984, 1985) help in the development of good comprehension skills. The model provides students guided practice in four different strategies: predicting, questioning, summarizing, and clarifying. Student leaders or student and teacher take turns leading the discussion of segments of the text using the strategies to support their discussion. The goal is to practice the four strategies so that the group can come to a shared sense of meaning about the text.

Modeling Comments

Read a short picture book to students and then model giving a comment about the book. It can be an observation, something that you wondered about, or something that surprised you. The leader then passes the book from student to student. Each student adds his or her own comment about the book to the discussion. Each comment should be something that has not been said before.

Visualizing

Learning to visualize while reading is an important skill for students to develop. Read Ralph Fletcher's book *Twilight Comes Twice* (1997) to the students but do not show them the pictures. At key points in the story, stop reading and ask students to describe what they are seeing in their minds at that moment. After the book is finished, have students draw one of the pictures they were seeing and link it back to the passage they were hearing. Discuss with students the idea that reading should help us visualize and make a connection to pictures in the mind.

Making Inferences

Students need to develop the ability to make inferences while reading. To help fine-tune their skills, give students a character grid with the names of the main characters along the top of the grid. On the side of the grid, place the words "qualities," "characteristics," "interests," "likes," "dislikes," and "relationships." Read a story aloud to students and ask them to listen for the information on the left side of their grid about each character. As students hear information that fits the categories, they write the descriptors under the character's name. At the end of the story, lists are compared and discussed.

Discussing Confusing Material

Give students small "flag" markers and ask them to place a flag in any areas where comprehension was lost while reading. At the end of reading, ask students to go back to the text with a partner to discuss the confusing material. The partners should try to clarify the passage and make sense out of the message. Afterward, both partners should write a reflection about what made the passage confusing and what strategies they might use in the future to figure out a similar passage without getting confused.

Fix Up Strategies for Comprehension Building During Reading

Students of all ages should also be taught what to do when comprehension is lost. We sometimes assume that students in higher grades know this but some do not. Instead, their "coping strategy" is just to avoid reading whenever possible. Teacher modeling of fix-up strategies is important for students so that they understand how to apply these strategies in their own reading. As you read to students, you can model this by saying, "Let me read ahead to see if that term starts to make sense" or "I missed that part. Let me rethink what is happening here" or "Let me reread this section a little more slowly so I can see if it makes more sense" or "I think I need to change the picture in my mind about what is happening."

For primary students, there are simple, easily taught methods that will help even beginning readers improve their strategies for comprehension monitoring. Steps for teaching good comprehension strategies to young readers are:

- Look at the picture for clues; make a prediction or guess about what the word might mean. Does it make sense in this context?
- Reread the sentence and see if it makes sense the second time.
- Read on and ignore the word and see if you still understand what is being said.
- If you come to a word you don't know, sound it out, say it slow and "snap" it together, or make a word substitution that makes sense.
- Ask for help from the teacher if you are still confused.

For English language learners, you must distinguish between mistakes in reading as opposed to mistakes in language. This will make a difference in how you approach the student's reading tasks. With English language learners you will also need to give more attention to the ends of words in initial reading instruction. Second-language learners often have trouble discerning that the meaning of English words changes with different inflectional endings. Use words with second-language students in the same formats as they are taught to the students. When the format or meaning of the word changes, teach the word again as a new word. Don't assume that the student will recognize this relationship. Explicitly teach both grammar patterns and the syntax of the language to students. Most languages differ from English in how sentences are grammatically constructed. This often creates confusion for the speaker of another language. Irregular verbs often give second-language learners difficulty because there is no pattern for them to follow with these words. Teach these verb forms directly to the students. When students have developed literacy skills in their own language, you can also tie the new learning to these skills. Many immigrant children are not literate in their own language so a different approach must be used with these students and building strong background knowledge will be essential for these students. These strategies will improve the comprehension of your English language learners and will help them improve both their language development and their reading development.

Establishing Reader Conferences

As students read fictional material, we should frequently make time to conference with readers about their reading. Conferencing not only gives students an opportunity to share what they are reading but it also allows us to help frame a student's thinking and check for understanding. This instructional approach works for all levels with modification of questions up or down to meet the needs of the individual learners. We can conference with students about their own reading by asking the following questions to guide their learning and understanding.

- What book have you chosen?
- What kind or genre of book is it?
- Did you choose this book because you like the genre or because of the subject of the story?
- Have you read anything by this author before? Is it similar to his or her other works?
- Has the book held your interest? How did the book start?
- Did this author begin her book in a way that you might like to begin a piece of writing?
- What has been the most interesting part?
- Have you read any other books that are like this one?
- Can you share with me a section that you particularly like?

Nonfiction text requires different reading strategies than does fictional text. Nonfiction text usually uses one of several approaches to convey factual information on the key topic. Just as with fiction, students can be taught to recognize the patterns of nonfiction and to anticipate how data will be presented once they have identified the organizational pattern of the text. Graphic organizers are good tools to organize information obtained from nonfiction materials. A nonfiction text generally uses one of the following approaches to organize the material: cause and effect; compare and contrast; concept with definition; description; problem and solution; main idea with supporting details; or a sequence of events. Helping students understand and identify the organizational approach of the material will better prepare them to locate and organize important information that may be presented.

Comprehension in the Content Areas

Content-area teachers often complain that students can't read their textbooks. However, content textbooks in the middle and upper grades are frequently written above the student's independent level of reading. Often these books are written at a high school or even collegiate level so it is no wonder that students find it difficult to understand the material. Some teachers think that the key is to buy textbooks that are "dumbed down" so that their students can read them. As adults, these students will have to process many different levels of printed material during their lifetimes so using simplified versions of the textbook only encourages students to remain unable to process high-level text. The key to helping students make sense of expository text is to use "before, during, and after" activities to prepare the students for the material they need to read and to assist them in making meaning from the text as they read.

We must select reading methods that maximize student engagement with the reading text. In content-area classrooms, teachers frequently engage in the practice of asking for volunteers to read the material aloud or going around the class in round-robin style. As has already been noted, the research is clear that this strategy neither improves reading ability nor enhances comprehension. We need to examine whether all students really need to read an entire chapter from start to finish. Isn't it the information and the concepts that we want them to have from the material? More effective strategies for content instruction that strengthen reading skills include:

- Read a paragraph or two and then stop to ask students to summarize. Students should also take notes on the summarized information.
- Use the high-level textbook as a reference and ask students either with partners or small groups to "locate" and identify key information and place it into a graphic organizer of some type. Students will then

have a clear understanding of the information that they need to locate within the text.

• Assign small groups of students certain sections of a textbook chapter to read and summarize. Ask students to read the section and be able to tell (show, put on the board, demonstrate, make a model, etc.) the rest of the class the important points the author is trying to make in the section. Students will then report to the whole group on their section. Other students in the class should be asked to take notes on all information presented and to ask questions of the presenters until they clearly understand the important points of that section of the chapter.

We know that hands-on, active participation in learning instills a greater understanding on the part of the learner. Instead of simply reading the chapter, ask students to participate in a simulation that will instill the same information. For example, when teaching a chapter on voting and elections, one teacher asked students to actually conduct a mock election from start to finish. Students were asked to investigate issues and align with political party affiliations, develop campaign platforms, identify candidates, advertise and campaign for their party, get voters registered to vote, and hold a mock election. While this simulation took three weeks to conduct, the student's level of understanding was much deeper and more personal than it would have been had the students simply read about political parties and voting and answered the questions at the end of the chapter. Instead of a dreary reading assignment that many of the students dreaded or even ignored altogether, the textbook became a frequent resource as the students were asked questions such as "What requirements are there to run for President in the United States?" Students then had a strong interest and purpose for reading the material that had been provided to them in their textbook.

The Internet is a powerful and mostly free resource for content-area teachers. No longer should we limit our students to one textbook as a source for all their learning. We should locate (or have students locate) additional information regarding the topic under study. We can also place students into different interest groups so that each group learns about a specific topic that they later share with their peers. For example, in the voting simulation, certain groups could have been charged with determining needed information on candidate requirements, fundraising strategies, marketing, voter registration procedures, and so forth. Each group could have then made a presentation to share the information. For accommodating students with various reading levels, the Internet is a good source for materials written on all levels of difficulty. When doing research on the Internet, students can then be asked to compare and contrast sources for accuracy and bias. The traditional textbook should be just another resource for our students, not the main attraction.

Students should be asked to summarize information, draw conclusions, create models, and make inferences from the material they have read. These are truly the skills that our students will need in adult life. Except perhaps in graduate school, how many times as an adult have we been asked to read a chapter of a book and answer the questions at the end of the chapter? Comprehension is enhanced when reading is shared and discussed, and when different points of view are considered.

When adults read articles, they frequently like to discuss them with other adults in an analytical way. For example, we might say to a friend, "Did you see that article on the state of the economy in the last issue of *Business Week*? What do you think of what it had to say?" We can interest students more in content-area information by also bringing in additional articles and resources on key topics. A subject area is much more alive when there is a spark of controversy or novelty added to the curriculum. As adults, we often take notes on material that we are trying to remember or make a part of our own knowledge and understanding. Students should be taught how to cull important information from expository text, even in primary grades. The format will grow more complex and the students more adept as they progress through the grades, but note taking is a skill that we all will use on countless occasions all of our adult lives, so it is a skill our students need to learn. In the most effective schools, teachers selected one uniform system of note taking and taught students this system schoolwide. It did not matter which system was used, just that the same system was practiced throughout the school so that students could be come adept at using the system.

After-Reading Activities

After reading a text, we want students to focus on clarifying their understandings and connecting the new knowledge to prior knowledge. We can help students verify predictions, organize information, and summarize, classify, or otherwise process the information at deeper levels of understanding. We want students to complete any organizer charts they started before or during reading, discuss their insights with us and peers, and perhaps link their new knowledge to a writing assignment. Some strategies to focus student attention after the reading has taken place include the following activities:

Coming Attractions

Ask students to make a poster, a set of transparencies, or a computer slide show similar to a movie's "coming attractions" format to showcase a particular book they have been reading. The "coming attraction" should be designed to peak the interest of other readers.

Summary Journal

Ask students to complete a summary journal at the end of each reading session. The summary journal should describe the action of the story, development of the characters, impact of the setting on the plot, comments on the author's style, or other ideas that the reader has after the reading selection.

Group Discussion

After reading, have students form a discussion group and give each group a large sheet of butcher paper on which to record their discussion. Each person is given a three-by-five-inch card on which is written one of the words: *characters; setting; theme; resolution* (for fiction) or *main idea; details; key words; connections; organization* (for nonfiction). Each student is asked to locate information on the topic given to them on the card and to discuss this aspect with their group. At the end of the discussion, each group is to make a graphic organizer on the butcher paper to show the key elements of the text they have been reading.

Writing Summaries

Teach students to summarize stories as early as 1st grade. Give students a pattern format that will help them glean information in a predictable manner. For example, ask students, "Where did this story take place?" Then ask, "Who were the main characters in the story?" After students make a list, ask students to identify, "What was the problem that happened in the story?" Then ask students, "How was the problem solved?" Teach students to construct a summary that follows a format such as, "This story took place in a forest. The main characters were a wolf, a woodsman, and Little Red Riding Hood. The problem was that Little Red Riding Hood wanted to visit her grandmother but a wolf was there instead. The wolf wanted to eat Little Red Riding Hood but a brave woodsman came and killed the wolf. Little Red Riding Hood found her grandmother locked in a closet and she was happy." Once children have been taken through this model on many books, they will have no trouble constructing their own summaries of books that they have read.

Brief Points

When students leave the class, ask them to write down a brief but important piece of learning or an understanding that they gained during the lesson. Stand at the door and collect the "tickets out the door." Students can also be encouraged to write something they still wonder about or something they still don't understand. We can gain a lot of information about what students found insightful or points that still confuse them.

Time Line

Ask students to make a time line of key events that occurred in the story, showing the sequence of when things happened in chronological order.

Character Traits

Request that students list each main character from the text and provide five adjectives that describe each character. Have students locate examples from the story to prove their point. Information and rationale should be shared with other class members to see if they agree with the assessment.

Story Pyramid

Have students complete a story pyramid after they finish a story. They should draw lines in a pyramid design and insert the following information from the story. Line 1: Name of the main character; Line 2: Two words that describe the main character; Line 3: Three words to describe the story setting; Line 4: Four words about the problem; Line 5: Five words describing the first major event in the story; Line 6: Six words describing the second major event in the story; Line 7: Seven words describing the third major event in the story; Line 8: Eight words describing the resolution of the problem in the story.

Prequels and Sequels

In pairs, have students read a story and then create a prequel to the story. The prequel should describe what might have happened to the characters before the story started. Later, have the same partners write a sequel to the same story. Have students discuss how inferences played a role in the creation of the prequels and sequels.

Writing Questions

Let the students "play teacher" by writing questions to give to other students in the class from a specific text. The questions can fit into three catagories: literal information covered in the text; information that can be inferred by combining information in the text; or information in the reader's prior knowledge base.

Reader's Notebooks

Ask students to keep "reader's notebooks" to record reactions to books, notes on teacher read-alouds, content information, or personal free reading done by students. Students can reflect on the impact of the text on them, their own personal reactions, links that they make to other knowledge, or other texts or questions that they have about the text.

The Importance of Genre

Fiction comes in many styles called "genres." Students should be taught to identify genres of text so that they can better understand the organizational format of the material they are reading. Being able to identify the genre of a story helps students learn what to expect in various forms of writing. Students should learn the characteristics of various genres such as fantasy, realistic fiction, and nonfiction and should be able to identify and classify what they are reading by genre. The following genres are typical fiction genres that students might read and examine:

- Fairy tale: A story about real and magical problems and situations often involving animals, people, and magical events.
- Tall tale: A story that contains characters with extraordinary or exaggerated abilities.
- Nursery rhyme: Rhyme written to amuse young children usually about daily occurrences or people or things common to a child's world. Meant to be read aloud or even sung.
- Folk tale or legend: A cultural story from oral tradition that has been passed on through the generations through repeated tellings.
- Fable: A short story that teaches a moral or a lesson. The story often uses animals as key characters in the story.
- Myth: A story or allegory passed down through oral tradition that explains such concepts as race, culture, religion, nature, or natural phenomenon.
- Pourquoi tale or "just so" story: A tale that explains the origin of everyday events and traditions.
- Play: A story written primarily with dialog to be performed by live actors before an audience.
- Trickster tale: A story written with a special twist or mystery that readers are challenged to figure out as they are reading.

• Science fiction: An imaginary story based on futuristic technological advances. Often set in space or on other planets.

• Fantasy: An imaginary story often set in the Middle Ages containing imaginary characters such as elves, dwarves, and dragons. Magic is often involved in fantasy stories.

• Mystery: A well-planned story containing an unknown element that the reader must try to solve, puzzle over, or discover.

• Realistic fiction: Believable characters and narrative story that seems as if it could have actually happened as described. Often has a strong protagonist, hero, or heroine.

• Historical fiction: An imaginary story or author's interpretation of a historical event. Main characters are real historical personalities and are based primarily on historical fact.

Many language arts teachers like to expose students to units of study around particular authors or genres. This thematic approach helps students identify an author's style and draw conclusions about how a particular author views life. This technique can also allow students to compare and contrast different author styles. Comparisons can also be made within a genre such as mystery or science fiction. Students who spend time studying in this manner often can pick up ideas for their own writing style. Reading from different genres also helps students find their favorite "niches" where they might continue reading as an adult reader. Students, especially those in early grades, love to reread the books that have been studied in class with their teacher. It is a good idea for us to place these books in a special tub or reading center area so that students can continue to reread them whenever they like. Another good idea is to make sure that the librarian has several copies of the books available for students who are doing an author study so that students can take the books home and reread them with family members.

Comprehension Is the Heart of the Reading Process

Comprehension skills are the heart of the reading process, and we bring our life experiences to the act of reading. As Pressley (2000) has identified, the goal of teaching students comprehension strategies is to have self-regulated readers who are able to apply a repertoire of reading skills both flexibly and appropriately in each situation they encounter. Using various strategies to help students before, during, and after reading is one way to help students better organize the task of reading and "sense making" from text. Teaching students how to expand their comprehension skills and monitor their own sense making will help develop stronger readers who are better prepared for tomorrow's world.

⚜ 6 ⚜

Higher-Order Thinking

When comprehension is deep and thorough, a reader is able to process text at higher levels of the thinking process. The reader is able to apply the levels of Benjamin Bloom's taxonomy (1956) and make meaning at more sophisticated levels. This thread is reading at the evaluation, synthesis, analysis, and interpretation levels. Good readers can monitor their own comprehension, interpret charts and graphs while reading, summarize as they read, make connections while reading, and process text after reading at sophisticated levels of thinking. Finally, good readers can remember and discuss in depth what they have read.

Evaluating information means being able to distinguish essential information or core concepts from what is simply interesting. It also means being able to discern a theme, form an opinion, or develop a perspective based on the information presented. Evaluation is the ability to make judgments about ideas and concepts being read.

Synthesizing information means taking new information and combining it with existing information to construct a new idea, a new way of thinking, or a totally new product or creation. Harvey and Goudvis (2000) tell us that "synthesizing is the strategy that allows readers to change their thinking." Synthesis is the ability to apply ideas and concepts in new ways. It is the ability to put two concepts together in a new way to form new thoughts, conclusions, or ideas.

Analyzing information allows readers to make comparisons with the information in their background knowledge. These comparisons allow readers to make generalizations about the information they have read so that they can form judgments and opinions. Analysis is the ability to combine a reader's background information and life experiences with new ideas or concepts to pull apart the information or concepts.

Interpretation is giving one's own "slant" or meaning to the ideas or concepts. Readers must take information from their background knowledge and make comparisons with known information to construct or "interpret" the information in a logical, analytical way. Advanced readers must be able to infer both implicit and explicit meanings. Readers can find and identify "hidden meanings" or symbols by linking what is known to the information they are reading. Interpretation takes analysis one step higher by requiring that the reader not only form opinions and judgments but also be able to cite viable evidence or proof from the work to justify a stance. Reading expert Laura Robb (2000) advises that students "need to be taught the complex strategies that enable them to appreciate the nuances of mood, tone, and theme in books. They need to be guided to make deeper text-to-text connections, so they can relate the elements and themes of one book to other books, to their community, and their world." The thread of higher-order reading accomplishes this goal.

Reading Application in Practice

In the real world, we use all of these higher-order skills to approach the reading that we do on a daily basis. As Richard Allington (2001) points out, we do not usually ask our friends to recall specific information from a novel they have read or a magazine article that we have shared with them. What adults generally do is ask others for responses, reactions, and evaluations of various ideas or information. We ask for our friend's opinions on the morning's lead news stories or his or her analysis of the latest trends on Wall Street, or we ask a coworker for her interpretation of a controversial article in our favorite magazine. We discuss novels we have both read and we ask our friends to discuss the perspective of a writer or the actions of particular characters. Despite the fact that this is how adults process written information, in school we often present artificial passages with little meaning or interest to students and ask them to answer questions about this material. Because this is not how we process reading in our own lives, why is this what we expect our students to do? We need to engage students in our classrooms in as much "authentic" and purposeful reading and discussion as possible.

Thinking needs to go beyond where the typical classroom now goes. We need to go beyond the basal readers to engage students in thinking and processing text at the highest of levels. To be prepared for the high-tech, fast-paced world of tomorrow, students must be able to grasp difficult ideas, analyze sources for reliability, and process many sources of information. Students must be able to analyze, synthesize, interpret, and apply the information they have available to them. Our students need to become literate "processors" of text who are able to use their higher-level skills to think, evaluate, analyze, synthesize, and make interpretations of what they are reading.

Duke and Pearson (2002) outlined six strategies that higher-level readers use to make meaning of text as they read. Those strategies are (1) prediction/activation of prior knowledge, (2) using think-aloud strategies to monitor comprehension, (3) using text structures, (4) using and constructing visual models such as graphic organizers and imagery, (5) summarizing, and (6) questioning and answering questions while reading.

Let's examine each of these strategies in greater detail. Rosenblatt (1968) demonstrated that readers use their prior knowledge, information, and experiences to make meaning from text as they read. He stated that it is this background that affects a reader's ability to comprehend the author's work. Minsky (1975) and Anderson (1984) later named this concept "schema theory." According to schema theory, each person brings a set of unique experiences and knowledge, known as "schemata," to the reading experience. Students with limited experiences and background knowledge have difficulty making connections to the reading and the material being presented. Because background is important to the reading process, we must ensure that students have the proper background knowledge prior to reading a new text.

Thinking aloud as one processes text is one of the most critical elements to building strong, higher-level reading skills. Encourage students to approach the reading of text material by making predictions about the material, testing the hypothesis made, and then realigning thinking as the reading progresses if the text does not match the reader's anticipated progression. Model text processing so developing readers can hear your rationale as you read the text. This strategy should be used with all ages to demonstrate to students how good readers handle each aspect of text.

Highly effective readers possess the ability to identify what is important in the text. Readers who understand the purpose of their reading are better able to distinguish relevant from irrelevant information in text. We must ensure that students are clear on the purpose of the reading so that they learn to use this information to guide their attention while reading. Researchers Billmeyer and Barton (1998) state, "How well a reader comprehends a text is also dependent on metacognition: his ability to think about and to control his thinking process before, during, and after reading."

Effective readers synthesize and summarize text in their heads as they read. The process involves determining the main idea of the passage and then relating the important key points that support and expand the main idea. At the beginning reading levels, the foundation of this skill is expressed as the ability to retell key facts or events from the text. At higher levels, students must be able to eliminate irrelevant or repeated information, categorize information into lists, form opinions, make comparisons, and make connections between points and details. Students must be able to take notes, outline the key points, and synthesize and summarize information in the material they have read.

Higher-level readers must also learn to analyze text and draw inferences from the text. Calkins (2001) calls this "reading between the lines" and "reading beyond the lines" to determine a character's motivation, personality traits, and story themes. Successful readers must be able to identify logical sequence and use the context to make logical arguments with supporting evidence from the text. Successful readers also must be able to identify author style, the method of developing the story and the characters, and interpret meaning through a character's perspective. Visualization techniques and graphic organizers help students sort out relationships and see the connections present in the text. We must help students learn to make these connections, analyze information, and support opinions and statements with text links.

Effective readers modify their reading rate and self-monitor comprehension. Proficient readers have strategies to use when meaning is lost while reading. Less-able readers, by contrast, frequently skip over difficult portions of the text or unknown words while reading. This action leaves them less able to recall or comprehend what they have read. Proficient readers have a good grasp of vocabulary and word meaning. They can identify vocabulary and word meanings at abstract levels such as with idiomatic or metaphoric language. They have good word attack skills and know how to use context clues, rhyme patterns, or word parts (prefix, suffix, affix, root words) to make predictions about the meaning of unknown words they encounter. For this reason, we must help students learn "fix-up" comprehension strategies (Pogrow, 1993; Caverly, Mandeville, & Nicholson, 1995) and ensure that vocabulary development is stressed with students in all areas of the curriculum.

Proficient readers pose questions before, during, and after reading. Questions help drive understanding and link old knowledge with new knowledge through analysis and synthesis. Modeling and using think-aloud strategies can help proficient readers expand their use of questioning while reading. Predicting is an early form of questioning that even the youngest of readers can be taught to use while reading. Questioning allows readers to sort out what they already know about a topic from what they still need to get from the text. It helps readers explain and justify their opinions and organize logical arguments as they read. Critical readers make connections while reading. They analyze what they are reading and synthesize the information in new ways. We must move beyond traditional "answer the questions at the back of the chapter" strategies in the classroom if we are to prepare students to be effective, literate readers. We must help students stretch and grow as questioning, thinking readers.

Skills That Readers Will Need for Success in Tomorrow's World

Some of the advanced skills that should be a part of student literacy instruction for fiction include examining figurative language and idiomatic expressions, questioning text, and evaluating the theme, author style (tone, voice, mood, and genre), and point of view. Students should be taught to interpret themes, analyze symbolism, cite instances of the use of foreshadowing, and examine character development in fictional works. They should be able to identify key elements of the story such as setting, plot, characters, rising action, conflict, turning points, and resolution. By the time they leave high school, students should also have a solid ability to engage in author studies and be able to compare and contrast both a single author's works as well as several authors' works in the same genre.

With nonfiction texts, students should be able to compare and contrast text, determine the reliability of data sources, and determine propaganda and/or bias in text. Students should be able to distinguish sequence, cause and effect relationships, and determine fact from opinion. They should be able to form their own supported opinions and interpretations based on data and cited evidence both orally and in writing.

These are complex tasks, but if we are truly to prepare students for the world they will face, these skills must be solidly in place for these students when they complete secondary school. We can no longer settle for simple comprehension for many and solid skills for only the brightest and the best. The world our students will live in requires the higher-level skills of evaluation, synthesis, analysis, and interpretation for workers to be successful. The higher-order skills can and should be woven throughout a student's educational career, and they are the application of all of the lower-level foundational skills that form the final weave. Higher-order thinking adds the coloring and the pattern that forms the beauty and functionality of the reading tapestry. We will examine each of the components of the higher-order thread separately.

Evaluation

Evaluation is drawing conclusions based on examining the information presented. Some examples of ways students can use evaluation strategies to organize data are editorials, panel discussions, critiques, or debates. When designing activities to strengthen students' skills in evaluation, you can use some of the following verbs to create activities that engage students in evaluation. The verbs most often associated with evaluation are: *justify, debate, recommend, criticize, summarize, interpret, conclude, evaluate, survey, challenge, defend,* and *weigh*. The following activities help reinforce evaluation.

Pair and Share

A strategy for increasing higher-level comprehension is to have two or three students form a pair and share group. Students share questions and ideas from the text with their partners, and discuss them in detail. Ideas and thoughts are then later shared with the larger group in a whole class discussion.

Wow! Books

Set aside an area for students to post summations of "Wow!" books that they have been reading. Students should be asked to list book title, author, and publisher and to give a brief summary of the plot and who might be interested in reading this book. Help students learn to write their summaries to include persuasive elements to advertise and sell their book to other readers.

Making Arguments

Ask students to find a part of the book with which they do not agree. Students must then find evidence to dispute the information and build a case for why they disagree. Arguments can be presented to their peers to "judge" whether or not they have been persuasive and logical in their arguments. This can also be a great activity while reading newspaper editorials or even to use with various magazine articles that may have a controversial slant.

Asking Questions

Students can pretend that they are the teacher and want to lead a discussion about a book. What 10 questions would they ask students and what might the students say in response to their questions?

Rising Action

Discuss with students the concept of rising action and perhaps read a story identifying this point in the story. Ask students to write a "cliffhanger" beginning. Students in the class can select the best beginnings and can complete various endings for the beginning. Students can take class votes on which endings they like the best to match the beginnings.

Sharing Facts

Before students begin to read a story or a book, ask them to think about a fact about the book that they would like to share after reading. They could look for the most exciting part of the book, the funniest part of the story, the most interesting part, the most surprising part, the part the reader liked best, or any other detail that the teacher and student decide on. After the reading, the students share their opinions with the other students in the class.

Reading Mysteries

When reading a mystery story, have students go through the story and identify key clues that the writer has included in the story to foreshadow the conclusion. Ask students to describe how the details work to build to the conclusion.

Synthesis

Synthesis is the ability to take information and put it together to form something new. Some examples of ways that students can synthesize information they have learned are by creating a pantomime, a cartoon or caricature, by writing a speech, or designing a recipe to organize the information. Other ways that students can synthesize information might be by creating a song, writing a magazine or news article, or producing a play or TV program. The following verbs can be used in assignments to help a student with the synthesis process relative to the material being read: *create, imagine, extend, compose, predict, hypothesize, compare/contrast, explain, invent, infer, improve, design, suppose that, produce, connect, outline, sort, synthesize,* and *categorize*. Some key statements that might assist you in designing activities that involve students at the synthesis level are: "Suppose . . .," "If you combine . . .," "Possibly . . .," "Imagine that . . .," "What if . . .," "I predict that . . .," "How about . . .," "I wonder . . .," "What conclusion can be made . . .," and "How would you summarize . . .," to name just a few. Some activities that engage students in synthesizing information include:

Outlining

Have students outline the introduction, body, and conclusion of the book or magazine article. Direct them to outline the same elements in their own story or expository piece of writing. Compare and contrast the results. This strategy helps students become more sensitive to the development of their own writing when they can analyze it against the work of a published author.

Letters to Characters

Direct students to write a letter from one character in a book to another character. Characters can be from the same book or from two different books for extra interest and fun.

Identifying with Characters

Ask students to identify one or two situations or incidents in a text that have happened to them at some point in their lives. Have the students compare how they handled the situation with the way the characters in the story acted.

Stage Production

Have students plan a stage or TV production of a particular book. Students should divide the work into three acts of two scenes each. A setting for each scene and stage instructions should also be included. This activity will help students better understand key details and sequence.

Interview Questions

Ask students to create five interview questions that they might ask the main character of a story. The students can also write the responses that they feel that the character would make to the interview questions.

Acting as Characters

Students can dress up as characters in the story who talk about the problems or dilemmas they faced. The audience should be invited to ask questions of the characters. Students should try to place themselves within the context of the role and answer the question as they think the character in the book might have answered the question. Props or costumes for each character would even add more fun to this wonderful activity.

Setting

Have students compare where they live to the setting of the story using a graphic organizer. How would a particular story change if it were set in their environment? How could a story with a similar problem occur in the student's own environment? What challenges might the characters face that would have been similar to the one they did face? For example, being "lost in a snowstorm" might translate into being "lost in a dust storm" for desert climates. How would the details need to change to accommodate this change in setting? Have students rewrite the story using the new setting.

Book Discussion

Tape and show students a book discussion from the Oprah Winfrey Book Club segments. Have students pretend they are Oprah and conduct a similar book discussion for their "studio audience." The interviewer can ask questions about the character's actions, ideas, and feelings during one or more scenes of the book.

Casting

Ask students to pretend that they are a movie producer and have a specific story to produce. What actors or actresses would they cast for each of the character roles and why? Students should be able to justify their choices and point to key details or information in the "script" that would support their decisions.

Evoking Memories

There are many books that evoke memories in readers. Try *Aunt Flossie's Hats* by Elizabeth Fitzgerald Howard (2000), *My Grandmother's Cookie Jar* by Montzalee Miller (1987), *The Button Box* by Margaret Reid (1990), or *The Front Hall Carpet* by Ruth Heller (1992). Ask students to think about the information in the story. They should then select an object that has memories for them and write a story about that object and the memories attached to it.

Family Stories

Every family has favorite stories that they tell about events that have happened to them. Ask students to interview family members (particularly elderly family members) about family stories that are important to their family. The student should collect and write down as many family stories as possible and assemble them into a "family historical records" book.

Pattern Books

Have students read simple children's pattern books and then write their own pattern books or poems using a similar pattern. If possible, share the books with younger children and revise the books as needed to make them more appealing to the targeted age group.

Higher-Order Questions

Ask students to develop higher-order questions to extend their thinking skills and have them place their thoughts on compare/contrast graphic organizers. Questions that might be used are:

- How is a glove like your hand?
- How is a dog like a cat? How are they different?

- How is a car like a bicycle? How are they different?
- What would happen if circles were squares?

Students could even turn this assignment into an essay or poem on the topic to really unleash their creativity and imagination.

Analysis

Analysis is being able to inspect, tear apart, classify, separate, and categorize data. Some examples of ways that students can analyze data are to prepare a graph, diagram, chart, or outline of the information. Analysis examines the various categories of information found so as to break down the data and make inferences and conclusions. Data can be examined and reported in many ways. The following verbs can be used in assignments to help a student with the analysis process relative to the material being read: categorize, dissect, analyze, separate, contrast, describe, classify, sort, break down, inspect, examine, label, infer, assess, and conclude. Key statements to assist you in designing lesson activities for enhancing analysis are: "The best part was...," "Compared to...," "What are the elements of...," "An interesting part is...," "What would happen if...," "Looking at this part...," "A logical sequence is...," "By contrast...," "By comparison...," and "What are the elements of...." Some activities that promote analysis while reading include:

Discussing Highlighted Passages

Encourage students to place sticky notes near the area of text where they have noted information they would like to share as meaningful during discussion groups. Whole passages that are insightful and shed light on a character's personality, thoughts, or actions can be highlighted. Students can then talk with their classmates to help clarify and deepen their own understandings of the text by adding their analysis to the discussion.

Setting Goals

Setting goals for reading is a good practice to teach students. Students could be asked to set beginning goals and then ever-higher reading goals as they accomplish the minimal goals for pages read per day or even chapters read per day. Students can keep daily graphs showing their progress on reaching their weekly or monthly goals. Students can analyze their progress relative to the goals they have set for themselves.

Author Techniques

Ask students to examine text for special author techniques such as the use of figurative language, foreshadowing, or character development. Have students place "sticky notes" in key areas to identify their findings. Findings are then shared with partners, small groups, or in a whole-group discussion.

Thinking Critically

Have students "be a critic" and analyze what the author could have done to make the book more interesting to a reader. Students might further develop this idea by writing a chapter, a new ending, or a new beginning as an example. Ask students to imagine a different ending for the book and analyze whether the new ending would have improved the book.

Thinking About Characters

Ask students to analyze which character in the book or story they most resemble. Students should also explain how and why they have come to this conclusion. Students can also be asked to compare the hero or heroine of the story to someone they admire. How are they alike and how are they different? Responses could be in narrative form or on graphic organizers.

Time Lines

Assign students to create time lines showing the sequence of important events of a story, book, or character. This helps students better understand the summarization process and helps to identify key details and sequence.

Solving Mysteries

Find short mystery stories that are written in a couple of paragraphs. Read the mysteries to the students and ask students to solve the mystery and identify where the author has provided clues for the reader. This activity will help students learn to analyze and make inferences.

Comparison

Compare two texts either on the same topic or written by the same author. Ask students to identify similarities and differences. Another idea is to compare a character in two different books such as a fictional spider to a real spider. How are they the same and how are they different?

Analyzing Sources

Students should be taught to identify bias and reliability in nonfiction material. Students should study a topic and identify reliable versus unreliable sources and prepare arguments for why they have classified various pieces in each category. The Internet is an outstanding source of articles that show bias or slant as well as reliable information.

Writing Editorials

Students study editorial format and then read several editorials, preferably on the same topic. Students analyze the position of each writer, listing strengths and bias. Students then construct their own "Letter to the Editor" on the topic, trying to create strong arguments on the issue.

Interpretation

Interpretation is being able to process information and apply one's own slant or viewpoint to the information. To help students learn to interpret, have them write a critique, a justification or opinion paper, or a persuasive paper. The following verbs can help you design classroom literacy activities that will promote student's interpretive skills: *make a case for, hypothesize, formulate, interpret, develop a theory about,* and *justify.* Some key statements for developing interpretive activities are: "My opinion is…," "I believe that…," "Based on my experience…," and "My interpretation is…." Some additional ways to expand student's interpretive skills are listed below.

Author's Message

Have students write a summary of the message they think the author wanted to convey from his choice of plot or story conclusion. Summarize three to four events from the text that led to this conclusion.

Imagining the Author

Imagine what type of person the author is based on the story he or she wrote. What would be this individual's likes or dislikes, hobbies, etc.? Ask students to cite information from the text that causes them to make these predictions about the author. Students can also use their imaginations to predict the same information about characters in the text. Again, evidence to support all opinions must be presented. Have students research the author's life. Do they still believe that their predictions are correct in light of this new information? Why or why not?

Rewriting the Crisis

Have students change the crisis in a story to the opposite crisis. Interpret how this change might have impacted the story. Is there another crisis that the main character could have faced or could this crisis have been solved in another way? Write about how this might have changed the story. Another idea is to have students rewrite the story with the new dilemma for the character to solve.

Critiquing

Ask students to play "book critic" and to critique a book that was read. Ask students to justify whether they were glad they read a specific book or they felt the book was a waste of their time. Students should provide solid justification and logical arguments for their assessment of the text. What were the book's strengths and weaknesses? Who might enjoy the book? How does this book compare to an author's previous works?

Interpreting a Character's Thoughts

Taking a stressful scene from a book, have students interpret the thoughts of the main character as the character has an internal debate about the problem he or she is facing.

Playing the Author

Have students take on the role of the author, and ask them, "As the author, why did you select the title that you did? What part was the most fun to write and why?" Students could even play-act on a guest author panel discussion where other students ask them questions regarding their featured book or piece of writing.

Rewriting the Story

Assign students the task of rewriting a story, changing the setting, time frame, or sex of the main character. How would this change affect the story? For example, what if Julie in *Julie and the Wolves* had been a boy? How might the story have changed? Have students rewrite a scene or book from another character's point of view or perspective. How might the story change? Would the conclusion still be the same? Students can also develop a compare/contrast chart to show how the original story compares to the new version developed by the student.

Interpreting Photographs

Show students a picture and ask them to study it for a few minutes and think about it. Then ask "outside the box" questions about the picture such as "What do you hear?" "What can't you see in the picture?" "Who lives here?" "Why is this a special place?" and similar types of questions. Have students record phrases that come to mind as they look at the image. Later, have students organize their thoughts into a poem or story using the notes they made from looking at the photo and listening to your guided questions.

Interpreting Characters

Students select a favorite character from a book they are reading and take on the persona and dress of the character. Students write a brief speech to discuss their own perspective or dilemma in the book and how they faced the challenges presented to them. This could also be a nice tie to social studies. Students could represent historical characters from a specific period in time, a particular historic event, or even a geographical region under study in geography. How would this individual talk, look, and think?

Keeping Journals

Students can be asked to keep journals about various books that they are reading as a way of keeping track of their thoughts, questions, feelings, or interpretations regarding what they are reading. Students can write about the book or even make illustrations of scenes, key characters, or points that are important to them.

Picture Books

Find wordless picture books and ask students to write the story for one of the books. Compare how different students interpreted the same basic story.

Storytelling Skills

Practice storytelling skills by asking students to reread a favorite story over and over again until they can retell the story to others. Encourage the students to use lots of expression and pitch changes as they interpret the story to others from memory. This is also a fun activity for older students to take "on the road" for presentations in lower-grade classrooms. Younger students love to hear the stories!

Cartoons

Bring in comic strips from the newspaper or political cartoons that require students to make inferences. Ask students to work with a partner or small group to infer the point of the cartoon and what connections are needed for understanding.

Higher-Order Skills Make Solid Readers

When asking questions, try to concentrate on higher levels of questions. Some examples of questions that will cause students to think at deep levels before, during, and after reading are: "What facts do we know for sure?" "What are we unclear about?" "Can you show the evidence?" "What causes you to think that?" "How can you justify that with your information?" "What do you think about what I just said?" "Help me understand how you got that idea?" "Do you see it differently?" "Can you find support for that in the text?" "Are you sure?" "What do your peers think about that?" "How can you help others think through that idea?" "How does this relate to your own life or to people you know?" "What don't we know about that?" and "What other information do we need?" All of these questions challenge readers and cause them to examine the text, the author's purpose and style, and their own interpretations of the text they are reading. It is through asking the tough questions of students that they will truly grow and prosper as literate readers and thinkers.

⇥ 7 ⇤

Frequently Asked Questions About Literacy

What Makes a Difference in Reading Achievement?

Krashen (1993) examined this question and determined that the amount of reading students do is directly correlated to their reading achievement. He found, however, that the amount of reading that students do in school (not including free reading or voluntary reading outside of school) decreases as students go through school despite the fact that reading skill increases. When we examine reading comprehension studies, 93 percent of studies show that students given more time to read in school perform better than students who have had high amounts of time dedicated to skill-building reading activities in school. Replacing more "traditional" instructional practices such as skill drills and skill worksheets with enhanced time to actually read (Reutzel & Hollingsworth, 1991) is well documented in the research literature as the most effective approach to building solid reading skills.

Collins (1986) examined the reading development of 1st grade students and also found a similar impact on student performance. Higher-achieving students spent 70 percent of their time reading passages, discussing what they had read, and responding to teacher questions about the material. Reading was a combination of active reading and silent reading. Collins found that student achievement was positively correlated to time spent actively engaged in the act of reading. Lower-performing students, on the other hand, spent only 37 percent of their class time actually engaged in direct reading. In a more recent study of effective 1st grade reading instruction (Pressley et al., 1998), students also demonstrated high levels of engaged time in more effective classrooms. Teachers in these classrooms used a balance of instructional methodology in teaching their students to read. These researchers observed that "classrooms of the most effective teachers were characterized by high academic engagement, excellent classroom management, positive reinforcement and cooperation, explicit teaching of skills, an emphasis on literature, much reading and writing, matching of task demands to student competence, encouragement of student self-regulation, and strong cross-curricular connections."

Time spent actively reading was identified as a variable in many studies of effective literacy practices. Allington (1977) and Biemiller (1977) observed that the students who were the poorest readers spent the least amount of time actually engaged in reading. Instead of actively reading, lower-performing students spent much of their class time on word identification drills, letter-sound activities, spelling, and penmanship drills. When these students read, it was often aloud to the teacher in small groups in a round-robin situation. These students often read only 100 words for every 400 words that their higher-achieving classmates read. Several studies show that more instructional time for simply reading consistently produced greater reading achievement gains in students, especially in lower-performing students (Keisling, 1978; Leinhardt, Zigmond, & Cooley, 1981; Taylor, Frye, & Maruyama, 1990; Morrow, 1992). Nagy and Anderson (1984) also observed that good readers often read 10 times as many words as do poorer readers during the school day. What gets practiced gets mastered. Students have to practice to improve in reading proficiency.

Foertsch (1992) researched the background factors most closely aligned to reading performance on the NAEP and actual reading instruction. His study examined factors such as instructional approaches, reading experiences, home influences, and demographic characteristics from student data collected in 1988 and 1990 at grades 4, 8, and 12 from both public and private schools. The findings of his research were that the amount of reading students did both in and out of school was positively correlated with a student's reading achievement. Despite research that shows that the most effective instructional approach involves extensive reading and writing activities, students reported inordinate amounts of time spent on workbook activities that had no positive relationship with improved reading performance. Those students whose families emphasized reading in the home performed higher than fellow students whose families who did not place such an emphasis on reading. Students had difficulty providing higher-level information on their reading, such as details and arguments to support interpretations of what they had read. Based on this information, increasing the amount of time for reading during school hours and involving the family in placing an emphasis on reading in the home clearly would help students improve their achievement in reading at all levels.

How Much Reading Time Is Enough?

Reading and writing activities build reading and thinking skills in students and go hand in hand to increase student performance in reading. The connection is clear—reading reinforces writing skills and writing skills reinforce reading abilities. Students at all levels should be engaged in either reading or writing activities at least 50 percent of every instructional day. Students are in school approximately 7 to 8 hours per day. Each day students should have a 90-minute block of language arts time where the emphasis is on reading, discussing, and analyzing all types of materials: basal stories, short stories, poems, newspaper and magazine articles, trade books, and Internet articles, along with linked and focused writing activities that develop students' writing skills. Reading and writing activities should also be done during content area classrooms throughout the remainder of the school day as well. Reading can be oral, silent, choral, or paired but it needs to be done actively by each student. Completing workbook pages doesn't count as actively engaged reading time!

Students should also be provided with up to 30 minutes each day where they can independently read materials of special interest (Allington, 2001; Cunningham, 1991). For older students, part of this time can be provided in the language arts classroom but much of this time should be spent in content-area subjects where students are given time to organize information and research special topics of interest within the content area.

What About Students Who Can't Read?

Students who have difficulty reading often do not understand how to go about the process of reading. We should model reading behaviors using many "think-aloud" strategies (Davey, 1983) so that students understand the thinking behind processing reading texts. In addition to hearing how to process text, these students need a substantial amount of time practicing at a level that is comfortable for them. Motivation also becomes a key to getting struggling readers to spend time actively reading. We must assist students in finding materials that are of special interest to them, at the right level of difficulty, and that they want to read. Having choice in the selection of reading materials can lend additional motivation that just may help the struggling reader stay on task for longer periods of time. Teachers working with remedial-level students should have access to a wide variety of high-interest, low-vocabulary materials for these students. Samuels (2002) suggests that teachers ensure that poor readers have assistance in selecting books that are at an appropriate level for them to read so that silent reading is beneficial for them. He states that increasing the amount of time students read helps develop the skills of word recognition, speed, ease of reading, interest, and comprehension.

Another option that can be helpful for struggling readers is for teachers to provide their own prerecorded special-interest materials (Carbo, 1989). Ideally, this should also be material in which the student has expressed interest and wants to learn to read so that motivation is strong. The student should listen to the taped material and read along with the tape until he or she can read the material in a fluent manner to an adult without the aid of the tape recorder. As the adult listens to the student read the material, guided coaching is provided to help the student improve his performance. The more the student rehearses the material, the more improvement he or she will make (Rasinski, 1990). Continued rehearsal and presentation of materials that interest the student will help motivate even reluctant readers to read for longer periods of time. The more the student practices and is guided by direct feedback, the more the student's fluency will improve.

Another technique that has produced significant reading gains in remedial students is to have these readers be "reading buddies" to students in lower grades (Cunningham & Allington, 1999). Because the struggling students must rehearse material at the primary level to present to the young buddies, they get additional practice in developing reading skills and fluency. The students have a high degree of motivation to practice material at the appropriate level of difficulty without feeling self-conscious about the material being too elementary. The reading buddies get together two or three times per week for approximately 30 to 40 minutes to share stories and writing activities. The struggling reader uses other days during the class to locate and prepare the new materials that will be read to the younger student during the next visit. The young children enjoy the individual attention and the older students gain direct reading practice at an appropriate level.

Isn't Teaching Reading Just for the Language Arts Teachers?

NO! In the 1970s, the "knowledge" database of the high-tech world was taking about eight years to double. By 1997, this number had been reduced to only four years. If this same exponential increase continues, by 2005 knowledge in the high-tech world will double on a daily basis. This rapid increase in the knowledge base of the world is predicted to occur as a result of the mapping of the human genome in 2000. Richard Oliver (2000) tells us, "This is the 'inflection point' of the bioterials era, akin to the completion of the periodic table in chemistry, the splitting of the atom in physics, or the invention of the transistor in electronics. With the explosion of knowledge that follows, we will conquer matter." The world that our students will live in will require the ability to process data at high levels and analyze, synthesize, and evaluate written information on a daily basis. Those without these skills will be relegated to low-paying jobs or even unemployed altogether.

Teachers in all disciplines must teach their students how to read, interpret and apply higher-level reasoning skills to their content areas. Teachers must teach their students the skills necessary to read and write like an "expert analyst" in science, math, social studies, business, and all other subjects the student encounters. Students of the future will need to know how to think and process written information because there simply will be too much data available in the world for even experts in the field to have at their fingertips. Content knowledge will be secondary to learning how to do research, process data efficiently, and use higher level processing skills. The real focus of reading instruction from 3rd grade on will need to be to prepare students to function in Thread 6.

How Can We Teach Reading in the Content-Area Classroom?

Reliance on a single textbook for any course does students an injustice and dramatically limits the amount of reading students will do in a subject. How can students be expected to read critically, process logically and learn to discriminate facts in the adult world if they have not been exposed to many perspectives on the same topic during their formative years? Because research finds that most textbooks are written two or more years above the average grade level of the students who use them (Chall & Conard, 1991; Budiansky, 2001), it doesn't make sense that this is the only source of learning used in a classroom in the content areas. Content-area teachers should use a variety of materials, including magazine articles, Internet articles, pamphlets, field journals, original source materials, picture books, photo-essay books, poetry, and trade novels. Isn't this what adults do in the "real world"? How many adults would think they understood all sides of a political issue by only listening to or reading one source? Too often, we simply present a great deal of information to students rather than asking them to learn and process a smaller range of information to greater depths. It is clear that "less is more and more is often less" in the world of curriculum and learning. We need to do a better job teaching "less" in a more solid way so that it becomes "more" for our students.

For students in 3rd grade and up, teachers must increase the amount of class time spent reading, discussing, and writing about content material. Where is the research that says that every student must read every word of a textbook chapter to learn the material? Again, perhaps the concept of "less is more" applies to textbooks as well. To increase focused, engaged time, ask different groups of students to read sections of the text and explain it to other members of their group or to other groups in the class. Have students in the class take notes on what their peers tell them. Encourage them to ask questions to gain deeper understandings. As each group reads the material, students can be asked to select an appropriate graphic organizer to sort and classify their information for presentation to the whole class. This also increases student's oral presentation and summarization skills. There is nothing that requires every student to read the entire chapter in a textbook to benefit from the learning. When small groups spend more time investigating and interpreting the material in greater depth, they will improve their information-processing skills and gain more knowledge.

Another helpful technique for the content-area classroom is the reciprocal teaching process developed by Palincsar & Brown (1984; 1985). This technique is a well-researched, successful strategy that can increase student engagement and promote higher-level thinking and processing (Rosenshine & Meister, 1994). Reciprocal teaching is divided into four components: summarizing, questioning, clarifying, and predicting. Students using reciprocal teaching work in groups and take turns leading discussions about the text they are reading, which leads them to understand the material better.

Other techniques that content-area teachers can use to help teach students reading skills for processing the data of their discipline are: graphic organizers; "think-alouds"; learning the key organizational patterns of the literature of the discipline; note taking; and applying knowledge in analytic writing assignments. Teachers in all grade levels and subject areas should also increase the use of graphic organizers in all classes. Graphic organizers help students visually and conceptually organize and analyze information as they are learning. They help students compare and contrast information, sequence important steps or events, show the interrelationships of concepts, and classify information. Graphic organizers can be used not only to present the key concepts of the discipline, but also to present the vocabulary necessary to process that content in concrete form. Students can also use graphic organizers to sort through information and make sense of data. Books written on graphic organizers by discipline are plentiful, so locating various types of graphic organizers that work for each discipline should not be difficult.

Content-area teachers should not take for granted that students understand the thought process required for learning content. We should demonstrate the thinking that is involved by talking through what readers should be thinking as they process data. Different disciplines organize information differently, so helping students understand the typical organizational patterns of the discipline is helpful to learning. As students are introduced to a content area, it is important for us to model for students how to approach the discipline. For example, students learning mathematics must learn to identify the organizational patterns and key words that are important to the interpretation of a word problem. A student must identify such concepts as "in all" or "what proportion of . . ." when they approach solving mathematical problems. Students will benefit from knowing that in story problems, the main idea of the passage is often found at the end of the passage rather than at the beginning. Social studies texts frequently use a "time line" or a "cause and effect" organization to present key information. We can model the thinking process out loud for students as we demonstrate how to approach a problem within the discipline. Pointing out these organizational patterns to students helps them better organize their thought processes when reading this material. Helping students identify important relationships will help improve comprehension.

When students go to college, they are sometimes overwhelmed by the volume of notes they are expected to take. Some high school students have done little note taking in high school and they do not have a good grasp of how to extract and organize key information that might be helpful to them while reviewing for exams. Teaching note taking and summarizing is therefore important for content-area teachers, whether they teach students a formalized note-taking system or simply have them make marginal notes. Students should be taught to summarize, synthesize, and cull important ideas from the vast amount of information presented to them. While reading, they should be taught to ask: Does this make sense? Does it fit with other information that I know about this topic? Do I accept this information as reliable and factual? Helping students identify and organize important information is also a bridge to better comprehension and learning.

Asking students to think analytically about important information in a discipline is also an essential skill that will be important to the workers of tomorrow. Students must be able to make logical arguments and support them with analytic data in writing. Today, data comes to us from many sources including the media and the Internet. Students must be able to take such questionable source data, evaluate its reliability, and make appropriate interpretations. Teachers in all subject areas must go beyond "read the chapter and answer the questions at the end of the chapter" if students are to learn to read information, process data, form their own opinions and conclusions, and respond in an intelligent manner. When we read and write, we reflect, evaluate ideas, and compare and contrast information with our prior knowledge. Students must become skilled writers able to evaluate, synthesize, and put forth logical arguments with supporting data to back their opinions and positions. Students should be asked to keep reflective learning logs and write notes, questions, and comments. They should also do formal, written proposals, analysis, presentations, and reports in content-area classes. This knowledge is absolutely essential to shaping the type of worker who will be needed in tomorrow's society.

What Should Language Arts Teachers Do to Teach Literacy?

In the language arts classroom, the emphasis on extensive reading and writing should, of course, be more intense than in the content-area classroom. This is the "laboratory" where students are expected to learn the art of reading and solid writing. In every language arts classroom, there should be extensive shared reading and writing activities taking place on a daily basis. There must be teacher-guided reading and writing lessons taking place with the whole class or in collaborative groups. Small group lessons guided by the needs of the students in the class must also be provided. Students must be engaged with the content and with making connections to their own background knowledge. Independent reading at each student's instructional level should be provided. Students should be allowed choice in selecting reading materials that interest them at least some of the time. Students should collaboratively read and write with peers on the same book or article or the same research or group project. Different groups should work on different levels of material depending on their reading ability and interests. The language arts classroom should be alive with performance and oral presentations to include reports, plays, skits, reader's theater, and reenactments. Print of every type—newspapers, magazines, literature, pamphlets, and even food containers—should be the hallmark of the literate classroom. Vocabulary words should be prominently displayed on bulletin boards or on word walls to surround students with the words of their curriculum. Finally, there should be an air of investigation, analysis, and deep questioning in the classroom. Students of all ages should be reading, thinking, analyzing, and responding to text in as many ways as possible.

How Do I Plan for Reading Instruction?

If we are to succeed in teaching students to read, we must first engage them in the reading process. Because reading is a participation sport, we must immerse our students in as much reading as possible both in the language arts classroom as well as in the content-area classroom. Simply put, students have to read to get better in reading. Therefore, one of the first goals of all teachers should be to expose students to as much reading as possible, at the appropriate level of difficulty.

The goal of teaching reading must be to teach comprehension skills and strategies, to develop background knowledge, to expand vocabulary and oral language, and to build understanding and comprehension skills. We must teach students how to approach all types of text, and provide motivation, excitement, and self-confidence to our students as readers. When adults read, we use many higher-level processing skills to make sense of the text. These skills include connecting what we read to our own prior experience and background knowledge, predicting and anticipating what will happen in a text, summarizing and making conclusions as we read, and developing questions regarding what we read. As successful readers process text, we also create images in our minds from the material, make inferences, and evaluate the material in an interpretive or analytical way. Effective readers have a vast repertoire of strategies to use as we read for different situations. Students who are learning to process print do not have this background knowledge and do not know how to vary their strategy usage. Therefore, it is vital that we explicitly teach students how to select which strategy to use and how to apply it with specific types of text.

Not only can we assist our students by providing modeling and guided practice on how to use the strategy, but we can also model our thinking as we approach the task. In many cases, students need to hear "thinking aloud" to understand why we made the choices that we did in our own application of reading strategies. After modeling the thinking aloud, we should then provide coaching and support for students as they independently apply the new strategy to text (Duke & Pearson, 2002). We will need to pick and choose strategies that are appropriate to the materials being read so we can plan cohesive, well-developed instructional lessons for our students that truly develop their processing abilities.

To teach reading effectively, there are activities that should be done **before** reading, **during** the reading process, and **after** reading. We need to keep these three time frames in mind when building literacy lesson plans for our students. Mini-strategy lessons provided before reading will help guide student skill development so that students can practice key skills in context as they read. Skills should never be taught in isolation but always in the context of immediate application so that students can link the knowledge to practice.

Strategies to Use Before Reading

The goal of "before-reading" strategies is to build background and make connections between old and new knowledge, introduce new vocabulary, preview or examine the material, make predictions, and help the reader set the purpose for reading. Setting the purpose for reading should always be one of the first objectives as we develop our reading lesson plans. Poor readers lack a vision of the kind of knowledge they are looking for while reading (Gambrell, Kapinus, & Wilson, 1987). For this reason, it is vital that students understand why they are reading a selection and what they are expected to learn or do as a result of the reading. What should the student try to learn while reading? How will students be expected to organize the information or what will students be expected to do with the information? Will students be looking for specific information to answer questions or complete a graphic organizer, or will they be preparing for a discussion on some aspect of the story or text? What students actually will be expected to do with the information will determine the strategies that they may need during the reading process.

Once students have an understanding of what they will be expected to do with the text or information, then we must help them establish groundwork and connect their prior knowledge in the subject with the new material to be read. For example, we might help students examine the genre characteristics or style of writing so that students see connections with other material of this type that they have read in the past. This knowledge will help them link skills and strategies that might be helpful with the text or information. Another example is previewing the chapter material to understand the organization or presentation of the material. During the preview stage, students might be asked to make predictions about the reading based on background knowledge, book cover, pictures, chapter headings and subheadings, or other relevant information. This will help students determine strategies that are appropriate to use with the type of material being read and the depth of understanding the reader is expected to have after the reading has been completed. We must also ensure that students are able to process the vocabulary in the text and that they can make sense of the material as they read.

Reading is the act of making sense of print. While some students pass their eyes over the text, if they have not gained meaning and understanding as a result of the act of reading, then reading has not taken place. Prereading activities get students ready to think about how they will approach the text and what information will be needed after reading. Here are some examples of ways that teachers can help students build background and make connections prior to reading.

- K-W-L or K-W-W-L charts (Ogle, 1986). Create a chart that has either three or four columns and label the columns "What I **K**now," What I **W**ant to Know," and "What I **L**earned." Prior to reading, students fill in the "What I Know" and "What I Want to Know" columns. A fourth column could also be inserted if you want students to insert a column called "**W**here I Would Find This Info." This is a helpful addition to get students to think about where the information could be found if it is not answered in the text they will be reading. The "What I Learned" column can be completed after reading.

- Probable passage (Wood, 1984). Students are given key words that have been selected from the text. For example, words that fit the categories of setting, characters, problem, solution, and ending might be selected from the passage. Students are first asked to examine the words and determine if they might be able to predict what the story is about based on a given set of words. Students are asked to write a paragraph giving the "gist" of the story. The teacher then provides a prepared summary paragraph to students with blanks for students to fill in with the key words prior to reading. When words can fit into several blank spaces in the narrative, students should be asked to justify why they have placed certain words into certain blank spaces. After reading, the students compare what they predicted with the actual story.

• Graphic organizer. Students are asked to create a graphic organizer to show what they know about a topic prior to reading about that topic. This is an excellent prereading technique for expository material. "Before" and "after" organizers are compared to show how much new knowledge has been learned as a result of reading the text.

Strategies to Use During Reading

Reading cannot take place without comprehension because making meaning from print is what reading is all about. Good readers predict what will happen in the text, question what they don't understand or what is confusing to them, and take responsibility for their own understanding of what they are reading. They think about and respond to the text as they are reading, visualize while reading, and connect the text to their own prior experience or prior background knowledge. They relate text to themselves and their own experiences, to other texts that they have read, and to what they know about the world.

Good readers are able to evaluate and confirm or reject predictions during reading and make new predictions as they read. Effective readers use the context, their understanding of language patterns, and letter-sound relationships to read and understand unfamiliar words. In addition, they use self-correction strategies for unfamiliar words or when they get confused. Good readers are able to make intellectual inferences to include generalizations and conclusions, separating relevant from irrelevant information, and self-questioning during the reading process. They can monitor their own fluency and use strategies to increase fluency with the given material. Effective readers understand how to see relationships and make connections. They can also examine the author's style, purpose, mood, or tone, and they can critique the quality of the author's writing, technique, or style. Good readers also take notes, make comments, ask questions, and summarize or organize the material that they have read. While most teachers think of students either reading orally as a class or silently as individuals, there are many ways that students can read in the classroom. Some ideas regarding ways that reading can be accomplished in the classroom are listed below.

• Paired reading (Greene, 1970 as cited in Tierney, Readence, & Dishner, 1990). The teacher pairs individuals so that a stronger reader is paired with a slightly less competent reader. Students can read aloud, sharing the reading task, or they can read silently, stopping at periodic points to discuss the text or find answers to questions that the teacher has provided to guide the reading process.

• Who can summarize? As text is being read, students or students and teacher stop reading and students are asked to paraphrase the key points of the text that has been read or the action of story from the point of the last stopping. Students can also be asked to stop at periodic points in the story text to make a prediction, ask a question, clarify a confusing point, or connect the text to something that they already know.

• Think aloud (Davey, 1983). The teacher models how to read and process the text for the students. After students learn the technique from seeing the teacher model this on multiple occasions, they can also be asked to "think aloud" for others, either in large-group or small-group settings.

• Pick a scene. Students are asked to mark their favorite scene with a sticky note as they are reading. After reading, students are asked to verbalize why they selected specific scenes. Students can also be asked to mark things that confuse them or that they wonder about while reading. These markings are then discussed after reading or at a stopping point during reading.

• Echo reading (Heckelman, 1969). The teacher orally models fluent reading for students. Students read the same material after the teacher is finished, trying to imitate the same level of fluency, expression, and phasing that the teacher exhibited. This is an especially good technique when there are many struggling readers or many English language learners in a classroom.

- Choral reading (Tierney, Readence, & Dishner, 1990). Groups take turns reading in parts. This is good for a poem, short text, or text where there is a lot of conversation taking place. Choral reading is also effective with "reader's theater" text.

Strategies to Use After Reading

After reading, the goal should be to clarify meaning, organize new information, blend information with prior knowledge, and confirm or reject predictions made about the material prior to reading. We also may want to ask students to recall and locate explicitly stated material, use the text to support conclusions and assumptions, or cite evidence from the text to support opinions. Students might also be asked to analyze or make interpretations of various parts of the text. Less experienced readers should be taught to summarize and retell information and to respond to reading through various writing activities that relate back to the reading. More advanced readers should be asked to think critically, evaluate the author's viewpoint, style, or techniques and make more advanced connections with prior knowledge, other texts that the student has read, and other world knowledge. Some ways to help readers make connections and links while reading are explained below.

- Prediction checks. Students check their predictions to see how many were accurate and how many did not fit the text. Students can complete any K-W-L charts, webs, or guides that have been provided prior to reading. Students are asked to discuss how the predictions from before reading matched the actual text.

- Maps or charts. Students are asked to complete any webs, maps, or charts with the appropriate information to show what they've learned from the text.

- Teach a lesson. Students prepare and present a lesson to their peers on information that they learned from an assigned section of text.

- Retelling. Students prepare a retelling of a story, either orally or in writing, to include the story title, key characters, the problem, and the main events. Retellings are presented in sequence and also include how the problem is solved and how the story ends.

- Draw the text. Students create a drawing of some aspect of the text. This can be a favorite part of the story, a favorite character, important scene, or some other aspect of the text.

- Act out the text. Students act out a favorite part of the story or present a speech based on a specific character's perspective.

- Writing connection. Students conduct a writing activity based on the text. This can be writing about a similar experience in the student's life (text to self), comparing the text to another text (text to text), or comparing the text to a world situation (text to world). Students could rewrite the text from a different perspective or point of view or with a different ending. They could also rewrite the text into a play, "reader's theater" or other format. Write about a favorite part, a favorite character or other important aspect of the text.

How Should I Group Students for Instruction?

In the past, students were often homogeneously grouped for instruction in core content areas, particularly in reading. We know that this practice was not instructionally effective and often did psychological harm to the students, particularly those in the lowest student groups (Kulik & Kulik, 1987). Flexible groups, where students move fluidly among various configurations throughout the school year, produce the highest learning gains (Fountas & Pinnell, 1996). A flexible group is formed for a specific purpose and changes members frequently according to identified need. Students might be grouped for the development of a specific skill, to accommodate student interest or choice, by work habits, by prior content or strategy knowledge, or by task or activity. Students can also be grouped to encourage socialization or simply organized in random assignments. In any case, students should be working with many other students in the class during instructional activities. Examples of activities that might be presented at the individual level are silent reading; listening to taped readings; personal reflections (recorded or written); journal writing; or research investigation. Some strategies that would be good for buddy pairs would be partner reading; shared reading; letter exchanges; pairings by skill to be learned; cross-age tutors; study or writing buddies; mapping and graphic-organizer activities; and brainstorming tasks. You can use small groupings of 3–4 with the following strategies: reteaching; vocabulary review and preview; read-aloud; clarifying ideas, events and questions; guided practice; summarization of material read; choral reading; chunking information into smaller segments; written response or reflections; or completing small projects in a group setting. Larger groups of 6–10 students make ideal situations for strategies such as big projects, "reader's theater," dramatizations or re-enactments, reteaching groups, and discussion groups. Activities such as direct instruction of a specific skill or modeling, silent reading, teacher read-alouds, choral or echo reading, and classroom discussions and presentations are best done with half a class or with the whole class so there is more participation to enhance the activity.

How Can I Obtain a Wide Variety of Reading Materials for My Classroom?

Budget restrictions are a common problem in schools across the nation. One of the biggest complaints that teachers have is that they do not have a wide variety of reading materials available to them in their classrooms. There are many ways to creatively locate reading materials at very little cost. Sources include: libraries, garage sales, student book clubs, used book stores, used book events, and donations. Another possibility is obtaining collections from retiring teachers. Print materials can also be teacher-developed or gathered as free pamphlets and flyers from the local chamber of commerce or even the grocery store. Parent-teacher organizations are usually supportive of purchasing books for the classroom and will often be willing to assist with various fundraisers for book purchases. Instead of sending treats on birthdays, ask parents to donate a book to the classroom library. Simple bookplates that list the donor family name can be glued into the front flap of the book to commemorate the donation. Don't forget that the students themselves can be a source of print materials for your classroom. Make class books and ask students to donate these "published" books to the reading center of the classroom. There are examples of good print for free in newspapers, magazines, pamphlets, and brochures. Parents can also be asked to donate old copies of magazines that may be torn apart and placed in folders for topic reading. Senior volunteer groups are often happy to help gather old books or magazines for teachers. Another source is the Internet. There are countless places students can do online research or download articles and informational print for classroom use. The Internet itself can be a rich site for learning about authors or various topics in which students express interest.

Basal readers are usually available for classroom use in most school districts. Many basal readers have some good excerpts of high quality stories. To encourage students to enjoy reading these stories, consider having students examine the stories and then rank-order the 10 most interesting stories. Stories that get high marks from student rankings should be considered important to read. Teachers can also have students rank order the five least interesting stories as well if they so choose. These would be last on the reading list for students. Some stories from basal collections would also lend themselves to being read aloud, particularly if there is a longer version of the story that the teacher can obtain for interested students. Teachers can also organize their instruction around broad themes such as "Courage," "Man Against Nature," "Responsibility," "Caring for Others," "The World and its Cultures," or "Mysteries and Dilemmas," to name just a few broad concepts. There are many stories, novels, and articles the teacher could gather around any one of these broad themes.

Another strategy to add interest for students when reading class novels is the "common theme" approach. The teacher selects four to six novels of various reading levels around a common theme. The teacher presents a "teaser" introduction to each book for all students. The books are then placed on display for a couple of days for students to examine in greater detail. At the end of the display time, students rank order the books according to their preference for reading the books. Students are told that they might not get their first pick each time but that the teacher will make every attempt to assign them to one of their top three priorities. The teacher examines the student preference list and then matches student interest, ability level, and number of available copies to the readers in the class. If the teacher is unable to assign a student to one of the first three priorities, the teacher holds a conference with the student to select a fourth compatible choice. Students are asked to write a summary, complete a graphic organizer, or answer guided discussion questions for various chapters. Students in the group are allowed to read the book however they wish. Some groups may choose to read the book as a group with each student taking turns while other groups may wish to read the book silently and independently. The important point is that the students, not the teacher, choose the style of reading the group wishes to do with their book.

How Can Teachers Use Writing to Build Strong Reading Skills?

Writing forges strong links with reading skills and helps children become better readers (Stotsky, 1983; Pressley et al., 1998). Classrooms should be filled with opportunities for students to write and to express themselves. In the early grades, environmental print, such as labels and children's names posted on desks and on classroom walls, capitalizes on children's natural interest in the words around them. Patricia Cunningham (2000) expresses the connection in this way: "Writing is perhaps our best opportunity for developing young children's print concepts, concrete words, phonemic awareness and knowledge of letters and sounds" (p. 23). In kindergarten, teachers must surround children with writing even when they are not yet capable of writing letters for themselves. Writing should be the highest priority after reading in the language arts classroom. Content area teachers can also link their subject matter to frequent writing activities to reinforce strong literacy linkages.

How are K-3 Literacy Skills Different from 4-12 Literacy Skills?

The primary grades are the foundational years upon which the more advanced threads of reading rest. Without a solid base, students seldom catch up with their age peers and reading loses its pleasure for them. For this reason, it is vital that primary teachers have a solid understanding of literacy development and that they know how to create a rich environment conducive to building strong literacy skills in their students. Primary teachers must be sure that the threads of phonemic awareness and phonics are solidly woven into the child's reading tapestry by the time the child finishes 1st grade. These strands must be "finished off" so that the additional strands of vocabulary, fluency, comprehension, and higher-order skills can be woven into the tapestry as the child develops more advanced reading skills. Several researchers (Cunningham, 2000; Stahl, Duffy-Hester, and Stahl, 1998) have observed that early phonics programs that teach letter-sound relationships coupled with invented spelling strategies produce better decoders than programs that do not include application of the phonics concepts in writing. Research is clear that phonemic awareness and strong phonics instruction can produce substantial reading growth in younger children in both reading and spelling concepts. This training, coupled with strong instruction in fluency development and beginning comprehension skills, will help children learn to decode more efficiently and effectively from the beginning of their reading instruction.

With struggling readers past the 1st grade level, phonics instruction is less effective. According to a National Reading Panel report (National

Institute of Child Health and Human Development, 2000), "phonics instruction failed to exert a significant impact on the reading performance of low-achieving readers in 2nd through 6th grades." Authors of the report suggest that there was insufficient evidence to determine the exact cause for the discrepancy in phonics effectiveness between beginning and more developing readers. They hypothesized that a possible cause for poor reading skills beyond the 1st grade may well be tied to poor comprehension skills and less involved with decoding skills. Nagy and Anderson (1984) explored the words commonly found in books from grades 3 through 9 and found that many of the words that older readers have difficulty decoding were polysyllabic and were related semantically. They concluded that older readers might benefit more from techniques designed to explore patterns and the morphological aspects of words such as root words, prefixes, and suffixes. Other researchers contend that sometimes struggling readers concentrate so much on the act of decoding that they have little cognitive energy left for attending to comprehension without specific instruction in the fluency and comprehension threads.

What Does Preschool Literacy Development Look Like?

In the preschool years, oral language and phonemic awareness activities should dominate the activities of the classroom. The goal of the preschool teacher should be to help students make the association that talk can be written down and that sounds correspond to letters or letter groups and words. During the preschool years, children should be exposed to many fun stories, particularly those with rhythm, predictable patterns, and colorful descriptions. The emphasis in preschool classrooms should be on oral language development, particularly with populations containing large numbers of low socioeconomic children or non-English-language speakers.

Preschool teachers should use extensive storytelling and teacher-led reading with students acting out key scenes from their favorite stories whenever possible. Preschool teachers should provide frequent repetition of nursery rhymes, poems, and alliterative songs, coupled with rhythmic movement. Students should be encouraged to invent their own stories and act them out during free time. An extensive array of dress-up materials and puppets should be available so that students act out different roles. Reading activities should dominate a large portion of the available preschool time with "favorite" stories being read and reread to encourage enjoyment and familiarity.

Preschool classrooms should concentrate on developing and expanding vocabulary through naming, repeating words aloud, identifying beginning or ending sounds, showing pictures and asking students to identify the beginning or ending sound. Singing "sound" or alphabet songs, doing word plays with alphabetic concepts, and tracing letters in a tactile manner with salt, sand, or shaving cream are all important activities. Orally blending and segmenting words along with the teacher should be a common daily activity. Because there are many wonderful computer games, electronic toys, and other games that emphasize alphabetics and letter-sound associations on the market, these toys should be readily available during free play and center time. Preschool children should be surrounded with oral richness and the sounds of the language.

Students should be introduced to using writing as a means of communicating messages. Labels and print should be prevalent in the play environment and the teacher should routinely call attention to these word labels. The teacher should be making extensive use of big books and easy books on tape. Students and teacher can write and "publish" their own "big books" as a class, with the teacher writing down the message students want to convey. In each classroom, there should be lots of paper and writing material available so that students can "write" anytime they want to do so. Teachers can and should ask students to "read" messages they have written but no attempt should be made to push students to write actual letters or words if they are not ready to do so. The focus for this level should be primarily oral with extensive exposure to oral language, including song and rhyme. Writing activities should consist of allowing students to "scribble write" or "pretend write."

The preschool classroom should focus on

- Exposing students to rich and extensive oral vocabulary.
- Helping students see that words are "talk written down."
- Helping students explore words, stories, and story concepts through play.
- Helping students build the understanding that writing helps us communicate our message to others.

What Are the Keys to Literacy Development in Kindergarten?

At the kindergarten level, much of the instruction in foundational reading development is still done orally through the use of ABC books, predictable books, and pattern books. The books that children enjoy are read over and over again so that children develop a good feeling for the lilt and flow of the language. The teacher helps students make connections to the reading and attempts to build background knowledge within each child's mind. Children are encouraged to join in to "help" the teacher read either chorally or in echo style. Just as in preschool, the teacher stops periodically to ask the children for predictions about what will happen next or to check predictions that were made earlier by the children. The teacher then skillfully leads the children to think about higher-level questions such as how they think the characters feel, how they would feel in the same situation, or what they think the character should do next. Discussions should be rich with new and varied vocabulary and the teacher should model using new vocabulary words in a context the students can understand.

At a later time, the teacher rereads the same book and asks students to focus on the phonemic or phonic elements in the book by asking questions such as "What words rhyme in this book?" or "Let's look at the words we see in this sentence. How many words start with the /t/ sound in the sentence that I am pointing to? Can you tell me which words they are?" or "Let's clap the syllables we hear in these words as we read the sentences." Students are given opportunities to represent the letter sounds both orally and in tactile/kinesthetic fashion. On some days, the teacher gives students a choice of which book they want to hear and the class favorites come back to center stage. There are many opportunities during each day for the class to sing songs, read poems together, and create and recite chants. Students help to create a class journal to record the important events of each day in kindergarten and do frequent composing of letters, stories, messages, and other writings as a class.

There should be many opportunities for writing in the kindergarten classroom, both teacher-led and student-initiated. Learning centers help reinforce skills directly presented by the teacher during directed lessons. Students learn that they too can be "authors" who can sit in the special author's chair and who can have their books available for others to read in the special reading center. A listening center or computerized phonics station helps students who have difficulty hearing sounds to focus on differentiating the sound as the sound is piped directly into their ears via headphones. At another center, provide manipulative letters and encourage students to make their names as well as the words they see written on the center backdrop. Instruction is focused, deliberate, and planned to meet the needs of the students and their developmental stages no matter how limited or how advanced each student is. The following activities should take place in the kindergarten classroom:

• Continuing to develop the understanding that writing is "talk written down," that letters represent sounds, and that sounds are put together to make up words. The words combine to create a message.

• Developing the concepts of print to include directionality, spacing, top to bottom, left to right, the concepts of "word" and "letter," and an understanding of the structural elements and organization of print.

• Expanding of vocabulary through naming, example, and explicit vocabulary instruction.

• Continuing to develop the concept of sound-symbol relationships, identification of the letters of the alphabet and their key sounds, and continued work with segmentation and blending. Students should advance from tracing letters tactically to forming them independently on paper.

- Encouraging students to ask their own questions about the text as well as to respond to each other's questions about the text. Noticing print features such as the word, sentence punctuation, or letters. Relating text to text and text to self. Using prediction prior to and during reading. Talking about authors, illustrators, and main characters in stories.

- Reinforcing all concepts and strategies used in preschool programs. Assisting those who lack appropriate background for kindergarten to strengthen their background knowledge. Ensuring that all kindergarten students leave kindergarten with solid phonemic awareness skills and alphabetic associations. Assisting with technology when beneficial to learning.

- Providing an extensive use of read-alouds, big books of all types, dramatizations, and labels in the classroom. Incorporation of games, electronic games, and computer programs as available.

- Ensuring that a broad array of writing materials is available to the students. Conducting teacher-led group writing projects on a frequent basis. Encouraging individual writing attempts with inventive spelling of words.

What Does 1st Grade Literacy Development Look Like?

One of the things that 1st grade teachers should do when their children first arrive in the fall is to ask them to write down all of the words they know on a piece of paper. Examining this list will help identify how that student has learned words and what words have importance to that child. This insight will be helpful in teaching the child to read during the coming school year. In addition to knowing the letters of the alphabet and their corresponding sounds, many students come to school with 10 to 20 words in their brain-based word bank that they can write.

Literacy activities should focus on learning how to match sounds, letters and words with the symbols on the page. Students in 1st grade should be beginning to read, process text, and write their own messages. Literacy activities similar to those of kindergarten but at a more advanced level are a major part of the 1st grade day. The 1st grade classroom should concentrate literacy instruction on

- Introducing more complex sound-symbols. Introducing sound-spelling correspondence and common spelling conventions associated with phonemes. Continuing instruction in segmenting, blending, and identifying phoneme sounds.

- Presenting sight vocabulary to students and continuing to expand the student's oral object and concept vocabulary.

- Creating variety in daily reading by including teacher-led, teacher-assisted, and independent reading.

- Teaching patterns to develop foundational spelling associations.

- Expanding use of comprehension strategies to include prediction, summarizing of the main idea, drawing inferences, and self-monitoring for misunderstandings.

- Expanding writing to include storytelling, journaling, and letter-writing, both in groups and individually.

- Continuing the emphasis on student enjoyment of literacy activities, active participation, and providing a print rich environment.

- Continuing and expanding on activities from kindergarten and ensuring that all students develop strong phonemic and comprehension strategies by the end of 1st grade.

What Does 2nd Grade Literacy Development Look Like?

At the beginning of 2nd grade, the teacher's first task is to determine which children have mastered independent reading and which children are still struggling. The students who have mastered beginning reading need to be provided with additional challenge and direction to expand their developing skills. The students who still need additional work in phonemic awareness or phonics and decoding skills should receive additional assistance and development in this area by skill need. Flexible grouping practices can assist the teacher in meeting the needs of the various learners coming into 2nd grade. Additional time with tutors or direct instruction will assist those students in acquiring the needed foundational skills. Parents should also be recruited to assist in the areas of need for each child still struggling to master needed skills. It is essential that every effort is made to bring students' skills on grade level as quickly as possible. Additional time to practice applying decoding skills and sight word development with easy reading material will help improve reading skills. Second grade teachers should focus their classroom literacy emphasis on

- Ensuring that all students have mastered the alphabetic principal, basic phonemic awareness, basic phonic concepts, and spelling patterns.
- Continuing to ensure mastery of sight words and developing fluency.
- Providing extensive opportunities for practice with reading, orally or silently.
- Ensuring that more advanced readers progress to an emphasis on comprehension by the end of the school year rather than on decoding.
- Beginning introduction to concepts such as compound words, punctuation, and meaningful sentence construction.
- Continuing all activities of 1st grade and expanding on them with the students at higher levels.
- Continuing introduction to strategies for reading expository text and the introduction of genre in fictional reading. Students begin to identify concepts such as setting, characters, story problem, and resolution. Introduction by the end of the school year to simple chapter books.
- Placing a heavy emphasis on modeling and developing fluency, ensuring comprehension and expanding vocabulary both orally and with sight words.
- Continuing with extensive use of writing and responding to text in all forms.
- Continuing to build students understanding of spelling patterns, syntactical relationships and sound relationships.

What Does Literacy Development Involve in Grades 3–12?

After a child has mastered the basic decoding skills for "learning to read" he must then switch his emphasis to "reading to learn." This is the emphasis that teachers in grades 3–12 must encourage. It is at this stage of reading development that teachers must ensure that each student is developing strong vocabulary and solid comprehension skills. Higher-order thinking and processing of text must now become a more prominent part of the student's literacy development.

Literacy Recommendations for Principals and Staff Developers

The following recommendations will help principals and staff development personnel quickly identify areas where additional training and support for teachers might be needed:

• Teachers in primary grades should be spending class time on teaching students phonemic awareness and phonic strategies and helping students expand their vocabulary. When students begin to read, they should be exposed to both fictional and expository text.

• Classrooms should be print-rich environments with many books of all types, children's magazines, newspapers, and environmental print such as pamphlets, food containers, manuals, letters, and flyers. Teachers should not be relying on only one source of print such as a single textbook, even in content-area classrooms. Students have different reading abilities and need a range of materials written at different levels to be successful.

• Teachers should be explicitly teaching spelling (particularly in grades 1–4) using materials organized around a word family and pattern approach. Teachers in grade 3 and higher should be teaching morphological relationships such as patterns, prefixes, root words, and suffixes.

• Teachers should be organizing reading tasks in all classrooms and content areas to include both "before," "during," and "after" reading activities. Teachers must ensure that all students are making connections with background knowledge and that interest in reading the intended material is being established prior to reading.

- Teachers should be helping students build strategies for reading with a special emphasis on prediction; summarization; asking questions before, during, and after reading; and extending and linking reading to self and other reading. Teacher "think alouds" can help struggling readers understand how to explicitly approach material that they are asked to read.

- There should be a high frequency of text-related writing and students responding to text and ideas. Students in kindergarten and 1st grade should be encouraged to use inventive spelling at the early stages of writing and allowed to transition to formal spelling as they are developmentally ready.

- Students should be actively learning vocabulary and working to expand all four of their vocabulary groups (listening, speaking, reading and writing). Students in upper grades should learn spelling patterns and root word, prefix, and suffix constructs to assist with decoding and vocabulary building.

- Principals should ensure that students spend a minimum of 90 minutes each day on reading activities. Content-area teachers should be using effective reading strategies with content text.

- Principals should ensure that students have multiple opportunities during the day to practice their reading skills. In order to read fluently, quickly, and with good comprehension, students of all ages need to actively read. Reading and writing activities should encompass a minimum of 50 percent of a student's instructional day at all levels, from preschool through high school.

Literacy Development and Student Success

Attending a school in which low achievement and low expectations for student learning are pervasive and chronic clearly places a child at risk for developing reading difficulties. Poor instruction in literacy during the kindergarten and 1st grade years may have long-term, detrimental effects on student reading development. Research by Pianta (1990) indicates that children harmed by poor instruction in the 1st grade year tend to do poorly across the rest of their school career. It has been determined that students with low socioeconomic backgrounds fall behind academically before they start school and during the summer months when they are not in school (Alexander & Entwisle, 1996). The rate of progress for these children during the school year matches that of higher socioeconomic groups at least through elementary school. For this reason, it is crucial that schools who serve low socioeconomic populations have excellent reading teachers, particularly in the primary foundational years, and that these teachers actively provide training on literacy development to the parents of the children they serve. Parent support and encouragement is an important factor in the literacy development of young children.

Building Successful Readers
Is Everyone's Responsibility

Students who are not on grade level by the end of 3rd grade have a slim chance of ever catching up to their grade level peers (Bloom, 1964; Carter, 1984; Shaywitz et al., 1992). For this reason, it is essential that principals and staff developers ensure that high-quality teaching is provided in all classrooms. The principal must also ensure that students are regularly monitored and evaluated for progress and that there is additional high-quality support for students not achieving grade-level expectations. In third-grade and above, students should also be exposed to prefixes, suffixes, and root words as an additional way of helping to decode words and expand vocabulary knowledge. Teachers should also be using graphic organizers, semantic maps, and extensive writing activities to help guide literacy learning in all classrooms, including content-area classrooms.

Teachers need to know how to choose among various strategies, work with various print forms, and create activities that support student achievement in literacy. They need to understand how to monitor student growth and what to do to provide support for students who do not master grade-level expectations. The principal must actively engage teachers in high-quality discussions about effective practice, literacy development, and achievement. Teachers also need feedback on the work that they are doing so that they, too, can adjust what they are doing to better meet the needs of the students they serve. Building successful readers takes effort from everyone in the school—from the building administrator, to the reading teacher, to the classroom or content-area teacher. Each educator has a part in helping students successfully apply and expand their literacy skills so that they can be better prepared to meet the needs of tomorrow's workforce.

⊰ Conclusion ⊱

Literacy is a complex and highly interdependent process that revolves around six basic threads. These threads begin to be woven in early childhood with the linking in a child's mind of "oral talk" and the funny symbols on a page of paper that represent that "talk." This early phonemic awareness allows the child to begin making the association that talk can be written for others to "read" or interpret into oral talk. Since this seems to be something that all of the adults around the child can do, the child becomes more and more interested in learning to read and asks many questions about this ability.

As children grow, they learn to decipher and decode the symbols on the page, and little by little they begin to understand that there is a separate written symbol that corresponds to each sound in our language. They then learn that these sounds can form words and that words can be put into sentences for others to share. At this point, children begin to make their own scribbles on paper, which they often interpret or "read" to any others who will listen. If the home is a literacy-rich environment, they will also be learning new words at a rapid pace and further developing their oral language and listening skills as books and wonderful stories are shared in the home.

When children enter preschool, they will continue to play with words in song, rhyme, and finger plays, and will expand their understanding that books carry interesting and fun stories that all can share and process. Hopefully, they will have opportunities to act out and interpret their favorite stories in "dress up" activities. They will also make new friends, both children and adults, who will further enhance their oral vocabulary skills. As children enter kindergarten they will continue to develop their vocabulary and they will begin to understand that letters have names and corresponding sounds. In first grade, children are introduced to blending and melding letters together to form words and begin the process of learning to decode the many symbols on the page. The teacher presents lessons about words and letters and talks about something called "phonics" that the children must learn. Learning new vocabulary words continues and the teacher begins to introduce simple books that the children are expected to begin decoding and making sense of. The weaves of phonemic awareness, phonics, and vocabulary are beginning to be formed.

As the children learn to recognize and decode a few simple words and sentences, the teacher models how to read the lines with fluency and expression. The teacher begins to talk about the words "making sense" as the children are reading. The threads of fluent reading and comprehension are now being woven into the literacy mix. The students practice their new skills and some words become automatically recognized and easily processed. The students read more interesting stories and continue to form stronger weaves within the threads of phonics, vocabulary, fluency, and comprehension. They also learns that books contain not only stories and songs and poems, but also factual information that can help them learn about topics of interest. Hopefully, some introduction to higher-level skills now helps them see connections between the text and themselves, other things that have been read, and the world in which they live. These threads continue to grow stronger as the children grow and the threads of literacy continue to be woven.

As the students reach the middle grades and beyond, they are expected to process text with a greater degree of comprehension and teachers begin to introduce large amounts of new vocabulary. Students are expected to have a storehouse of knowledge that continues to strengthen and be able to make strong connections between content, background knowledge, and new learning. They are now expected to summarize, discuss, synthesize, evaluate, analyze, and interpret the material (both fiction and nonfiction) that they are reading. The foundational threads must now be thick and strong so that more time can be spent expanding the students' ability to process data at the higher levels. The students are now literate readers, processors, and thinkers, ready to take their place in the society of tomorrow.

While there are many students who do indeed fit the developmental pattern of "literate readers, processors, and thinkers" emerging from our schools today, there are far too many students who leave our system without these foundational skills. Some of these students become so disillusioned that they drop out and do not even complete their education. Others complete high school but still do not have enough of a solid foundation in literacy to ensure that they will have more than a minimum-wage job in their future. Some come from low-income backgrounds where low literacy achievement is generational. Others are non-English speakers who have come to our country for a more productive life. Being able to read and process information is the key to an information society. We must raise the bar and ensure that all students have the background and training they need to lead productive lives.

For too long, the act of reading has been a mysterious process that was relegated to a school's reading or language arts teachers. As teachers, we must all understand that the threads underlying effective reading must work to ensure that all of our students master the techniques needed to read the content of our discipline. We must organize our lessons around "before," "during," and "after" reading segments and must help our students think critically, creatively, and deliberately in all content areas, from math, to social studies, to science. We must engage students in high concentrations of reading and writing throughout the school day and across all disciplines. We must help students plan for reading, engage in active reading, and debrief with others to add depth and breadth to their level of comprehension. We must excite and motivate readers and weave the threads tightly and solidly in our students. Reading permeates all that we do. Our abilities in this area often determine what we will be able to do and become in life. Let the threads of reading be solidly woven into our classrooms, our lessons, and above all, our students.

⚜ References ⚛

Adams, M. J. (1990). *Beginning to read: Thinking and learning about print.* Cambridge, MA: M.I.T. Press.

Adams, M. J., Foorman, B. R., Lundberg, I., & Beeler, T. (1996). *Phonemic awareness in young children.* Baltimore: Brookes Publishing Co.

Adams, M. J., Foorman, B. R., Lundberg, I., & Beeler, T. (1998). The elusive phoneme: Why phonemic awareness is so important and how to help children develop it. *American Educator, 22*(1–2), 18–29.

Alexander, K. L. & Entwisle, D. R. (1996). Family type and children's growth in reading and math over the primary grades. *Journal of Marriage and the Family 58*(2), 341–55.

Allington, R. (1977). If they don't read much, how are they ever gonna get good? *Journal of Reading, 21,* 57–61.

Allington, R. (1980). Poor readers don't get to read much in reading groups. *Language Arts, 57,* 872–877.

Allington, R. (1983). Fluency: The neglected goal. *Reading Teacher, 36,* 556–561.

Allington, R. (2001). *What really matters for struggling readers.* New York: Addison-Wesley Educational Publishers.

Anders, P., Bos, C. & Filip, D. (1984). The effect of semantic feature analysis on the reading comprehension of learning-disabled students. In J. A. Niles & L.A. Harris (Eds.), *Changing perspectives on research in reading/language processing and instruction.* Rochester, NY: National Reading Conference.

Anderson, R. (1984). Role of reader's schema in comprehension, learning and memory. In R. Anderson, J. Osborne, & R. Tierney (Eds.), *Learning to read in American schools.* Hillsdale, NJ: Erlbaum.

Anderson, R., Hiebert, E., Scott, J., & Wilkinson, I. (1985). *Becoming a Nation of Readers: The Report of the Commission on Reading.* Washington, DC: National Academy of Education, Commission on Education and Public Policy.

Aram, D. M, & Hall, N. E. (1989). Longitudinal follow-up of children with preschool communication disorders: Treatment implications. *School Psychology Review, 18*(4), 487–501.

Armbruster, B. B., Lehr, F., & Osborn, J. (2001). *Put reading first: The research building blocks for teaching children to read: Kindergarten through grade 3.* Washington, DC: The Partnership for Reading.

Beck, I. L., & McKeown, M. G. (1998). Comprehension: The sine qua non of reading. In S. Patton & M. Holmes (Eds.), *The keys to literacy* (pp. 28–36). Washington, DC: Council for Basic Education.

Biemiller, A. (1977). Relationships between oral reading rates for letters, words, and simple text in the development of reading achievement. *Reading Research Quarterly, 13,* 223–253.

Billmeyer, R., & Barton, M. L. (1998). *Teaching reading in the content areas: If not me, then who?* Alexandria, VA: Association for Supervision and Curriculum Development.

Blachman, B. A. (1991). An alternative classroom reading program for learning disabled and other low-achieving children. In W. Ellis (Ed.), *Intimacy with language: A forgotten basic in teacher education* (pp. 49–55). Baltimore: Orton Dyslexia Society.

Bloom, B. (1956). *Taxonomy of educational objectives: Handbook I: Cognitive domain.* New York: David McKay.

Bloom, B. (1964). *Stability and change in human characteristics.* New York: Wiley.

Brashir, A. S., & Scavuzzo, A. (1992). Children with language disorders: Natural history and academic success. *Journal of Learning Disabilities 25,*(1), 53–65.

Brown, M. W. (1947). *Goodnight moon.* New York: Harper and Row.

Brown, M. W. (1999). *The important book.* New York: HarperCollins.

Brown, R., & Cazden, C. (1965). *Environmental assistance to the child's acquisition of grammar.* Unpublished doctoral dissertation, Harvard University.

Budiansky, S. (2001). The trouble with textbooks. *Prism, 10*(6), 24–27.

Calkins, L. M. (2001). *The art of teaching reading.* New York: Addison-Wesley Educational Publishers.

Campbell, J. R., Humbo, C. M., & Mazzeo, J. (1999). *NAEP 1999 trends in academic progress: Three decades of student performance.* Washington, DC: National Center for Education Statistics, 2000.

Carbo, M. (1989). *How to record books for maximum reading gains.* New York: National Reading Styles Institute.

Carle, E. (1996). *I see a song.* New York: Scholastic.

Carter, L. F. (1984). The sustaining effects study of compensatory and elementary education. *Educational Researcher, 13*(7): 4–13.

Caverly, D. C., Mandeville, T. F., & Nicholson, S. A. (1995). PLAN: A study-reading strategy for informational text. *Journal of Adolescent & Adult Literacy, 39*(3), 190–199.

Chall, J. S. (1987). Two vocabularies for reading: Recognition and meaning. In M. G. McKeown & M. E. Curtis (Eds.), *The nature of vocabulary acquisition* (pp. 1-17). Hillsdale, NJ: Earlbaum.

Chall, J. S. & Conard, S. S. (1991). *Should textbooks challenge students?* New York: Teachers College Press.

Chinn, C. A., Waggoner, M. A., Anderson, R. C., Schommer, M., & Wilkinson, I. (1993). Situated actions during reading lessons: A microanalysis of oral reading error episodes. *American Educational Research Journal, 30,* 361–392.

Christelow, E. (1990). *5 little monkeys jumping on the bed.* New York: Scott Foresman.

Clay, M. M. (1972). *The early detection of reading difficulties.* Auckland, NZ: Heinemann.

Clay, M. M. (1991). *Becoming literate: The construction of inner control.* Portsmouth, NH: Heinemann.

Clay, M. M. (1993). *An observation survey of early literacy achievement.* Auckland, NZ: Heinemann.

Collins, J. (1986). Differential instruction in reading groups. In J. Cook-Gumperez (Ed.), *The social construction of literacy* (pp. 117–137). New York: Cambridge University Press.

Cowley, J. (1987). *Mrs. Wishy-Washy.* Bothall, WA: The Wright Group.

Cunningham, P. M. (1991). *Phonics they use.* New York: HarperCollins.

Cunningham, P. M. (2000). *Phonics they use.* (3rd ed.). New York: Longman.

Cunningham, P. M., & Allington, R. L. (1999). *Classrooms that work: They can all read and write.* New York: Addison-Wesley Longman.

Davey, B. (1983). Think-aloud: Modeling the cognitive processes of reading comprehension. *Journal of Reading, 27* (1), 44-47.

Duke N. K., & Pearson, P. D. (2002). Effective practices for developing reading comprehension. In A. E. Farstrup & S. J. Samuels (Eds.), *What research has to say about reading instruction* (3rd ed., pp. 205–242). Newark, DE: International Reading Association.

Eldredge, J. L., Reutzel, D. R., & Hollingsworth, P. M. (1996). Comparing the effectiveness of two oral reading practices: Round-robin reading and the shared book experience. *Journal of Literacy Research, 28*(2), 201–205.

Elliott-Faust, D. J., & Pressley, M. (1986). How to teach comparison processing to increase children's short- and long-term listening comprehension monitoring. *Journal of Educational Psychology, 78,* 27–33.

Ferreiro, E., & Teberosky, A. (1982). *Literacy before schooling* (K. G. Castro, Trans.). Exeter, NH: Heinemann.

Flack, M. (1985). *Angus and the cat.* New York: Scholastic Books.

Fletcher, R. (1997). *Twilight comes twice.* New York: Houghton Mifflin.

Foertsch, M.A. (1992). *Reading in and out of school: Achievement of American students in grades 4, 8, and 12 in 1989–90.* Washington, DC: National Center for Educational Statistics.

Fountas, I., & Pinnell, G. S. (1996). *Guided reading: Good first teaching for all children.* Portsmouth, NH: Heinemann.

Gambrell, L., Kapinus, B. A., & Wilson, R. M. (1987). Using mental imagery and summarization to achieve independence in comprehension. *Journal of Reading, 30,* 638–642.

Gillet, J. W., & Temple, C. (1990). *Understanding reading problems: Assessment and instruction* (3rd ed.). New York: Longman.

Gobran, A. (1978). *Intermediate algebra* (2nd ed.). Boston: Prindle, Weber and Schmidt.

Goodman, Y. M., & Burke, C. L. (1972). *Reading miscue inventory: Procedure for diagnosis and evaluation.* Katonah, New York: Richard C. Owen.

Goswami, U., Thomson, J., Richardson, U., Stainthorp, R., Hughes, D., Rosen, S., & Scott, S. K. (2002). Amplitude envelope onsets and developmental dyslexia: A new hypothesis. *Proceedings of the National Academy of Sciences, USA, 99,* 10911-10916.

Gunning, T. G. (1996). *Creating reading instruction for all children.* New York: Allyn and Bacon.

Gwynne, F. (1970). *Chocolate moose for dinner.* New York: Simon and Schuster.

Gwynne, F. (1970). *The king who rained.* New York: Simon and Schuster.

Hall, S. (1990). *Using picture storybooks to teach literary devices.* Phoenix, AZ: Oryx Press.

Hammill, D. D., & McNutt, G. (1980). Language abilities and reading: A review of the literature on their relationship. *Elementary School Journal 80*(5), 269–277.

Harvey, S., & Goudvis, A. (2000). *Strategies that work: Teaching comprehension to enhance understanding.* York, Maine: Stenhouse Publishers.

Hasbrouck, J. E., & Tindal, G. (1992). Curriculum-based oral reading fluency norms for students in grades 2 though 5. *Teaching Exceptional Children, 24*(3), 41-44.

Heckelman, R. G. (1969). A neurological-impress method of remedial-reading instruction. *Academic Therapy,* 4, 277-282.

Heimlich, J. E., & Pittelman, S. D. (1986). *Semantic mapping: Classroom applications.* Newark, DE: International Reading Association.

Heller, N. (1992). *The front hall carpet.* New York: Harper Collins.

Hoffman, P. M., Cunningham, J. W., Cunningham, P. M., & Yopp, H. (1998). *Phonemic awareness and the teaching of reading.* Newark, DE: International Reading Association.

Hoffman, J. V., O'Neal, S. F., Kastler, L., Coements, R., Segel, K., & Nash, M. (1984). Guided oral reading and miscue focused verbal feedback in second grade classrooms. *Reading Research Quarterly, 19,* 367–384.

Howard, E. F. (2000). *Aunt Flossie's hats*. New York: Houghton Mifflin. reading. *Reading Research Quarterly, 20*, 134–152.

Johns, J. L, & Lenski, S. D. (2001). *Improving reading strategies and resources*. Dubuque, IA: Kendall/Hunt.

Johnson, D. D., Toms-Bronowski, S., & Pittelman, S. D. (1982). *An investigation of the effectiveness of semantic mapping and semantic feature analysis with intermediate grade level students (Program Rep. No. 83–3)*. Madison, WI: Wisconsin Center for Education Research, University of Wisconsin.

Juel, C. (1991). Beginning reading. In R. Barr, M. L. Kamil, P. B. Mosenthal, & P. D. Pearson (Eds.), *Handbook of reading research, Vol. 2* (pp. 759–788). Mahwah, NJ: Erlbaum.

Juel, C., and Roper-Schneider, D. (1985). The influence of basal readers on first grade reading. *Reading Research Quarterly, 20*, 134-152.

Keene, E. L., & Zimmerman, S. (1997). *Mosaic of thought: Teaching comprehension in a reader's workshop*. Portsmouth, NH: Heinemann.

Keisling, H. (1978). Productivity of instructional time by mode of instruction for students at varying levels of reading skill. *Reading Research Quarterly, 13*, 554–582.

Keller, N. (1992). *The front hall carpet*. New York: Greenwillow Books.

Krashen, S. D. (1993). *Every person a reader*. Culver City, CA: Language Education Associates.

Kulik, J. A. & Kulik, C. L. C. (1987). Effects of ability grouping on student achievement. *Equity and Excellence, 23*, 22–30.

Leinhardt, G., Zigmond, N., & Cooley, W. W. (1981). Reading instruction and its effects. *American Educational Research Journal, 18*, 343–361.

Leung, C. B. (1992). Effects of word-related variables on vocabulary growth repeated read-aloud events. In C. K. Kinzer & D. J. Leu (Eds.), *Literacy research, theory, and practice: Views from many perspectives: Forty-first Yearbook of the National Reading Conference* (pp. 491–498). Chicago: National Reading Conference.

Liberman, I. Y., Rubin, H., Duques, S., & Carlisle, J. (1985). Linguistic abilities and spelling proficiency in kindergartners and adult poor spellers. In D. B. Gray & J. F. Kavanaugh (Eds.), *Biobehavioral measures of dyslexia* (pp. 163–176). Timonium, MD: York Press.

Lundberg, I., Frost, J., & Petersen, O. (1988). Effects of an extensive program for stimulating phonological awareness in preschool children. *Reading Research Quarterly, 23*, 264–284.

Lyon, G. R. (1998). Overview of reading and literacy research. In S. Patton and M. Holmes (Eds.), *The keys to literacy* (pp. 1-10). Washington, DC: Council for Basic Education.

Martin, B., Jr. (1970). *Brown bear, brown bear, what do you see?* New York: Holt.

Marzolf, D. P., & De Loache, J. S. (1994). Transfer in young children's understanding of spatial representations. *Child Development, 65,* 1–15.

Miller, G. E. (1985). The effects of general and specific self-instruction training on children's comprehension monitoring performances during reading. *Reading Research Quarterly, 20,* 616–628.

Miller, M. (1987). *My grandmother's cookie jar.* New York: Putnam Publishing Group.

Minsky, M. (1975). A framework for representing knowledge. In P. H. Winston (Ed.), *The psychology of computer vision* (pp. 211-277). New York: McGraw-Hill.

Morris, D., & Perney, J. (1984). Validity and reliability of the vowel matching test. *Educational and Psychological Measurement, 44*(2), 359–63.

Morrow, L. M. (1992). The impact of a literature-based program on literacy achievement, use of literature, and attitudes of children from minority backgrounds. *Reading Research Quarterly, 27*(3), 250–275.

Nagy, W. E., & Anderson, R. C. (1984). How many words are there in printed school English? *Reading Research Quarterly, 19,* 304–330.

Nagy, W. E., & Scott, J. A. (2000).Vocabulary processes. In M. L. Kamil, P. B. Mosenthal, P. D. Pearson, & R. Barr (Eds.), *Handbook of Reading Research* (Vol 3, pp. 269-284). Mahway, NJ: Earlbaum.

National Institute of Child Health and Human Development. (2000). *Report of the National Reading Panel. Teaching children to read: An evidence-based assessment of the scientific research literature on reading and its implications for reading instruction* (NIH Publication No. 00-4769). Washington, DC: U.S. Government Printing Office.

Ogle, D. (1986). K-W-L: A teaching model that develops active reading of expository text. *The Reading Teacher, 39,* 564-570.

Oliver, R. W. (2000). *The coming biotech age.* New York: McGraw-Hill.

Palincsar, A. S., & Brown, A. L. (1984). Reciprocal teaching of comprehension fostering and comprehension monitoring activities. *Cognition and Instruction, 1*(2), 117–175.

Palincsar, A. S., & Brown, A. L. (1985). Reciprocal teaching: Activities to promote reading with your mind. In T. L. Harris & E. J. Cooper (Eds.), *Reading, thinking and concept development: Strategies for the classroom.* New York: The College Board.

Palincsar, A. S., Brown, A. L., & Campione, J. C. (1984). First-grade dialogues for knowledge acquisition and use. In E. Forman, N. Minick, & C. A. Stone (Eds.), *Contexts for learning: Sociocultural dynamics in children's development* (pp. 43-57), New York: Oxford University Press.

Paris, S. G., Cross, D. R., & Lipson, M. Y. (1984). Informed strategies for learning: A program to improve children's reading awareness and comprehension. *Journal of Educational Psychology, 76,* 1239–1252.

Parish, P. (1963). *Amelia Bedelia.* New York: Harper and Row.

Pearson, P. D., Dole, J. A., Duffy, G. G. & Roehler, L. R. (1992). Developing expertise in reading comprehension. In A. E. Farstup, & S. J. Samuels (Eds.), *What research has to say about reading instruction*, 2nd ed. Newark, DE: International Reading Association.

Pearson, P. D., Hansen, J., & Gordon, C. (1979). The effect of background knowledge on young children's comprehension of explicit and implicit information. *Journal of Reading Behavior, 11*(3), 201–210.

Pianta, R. C. (1990). Widening the debate on educational reform: Prevention as a viable alternative. *Exceptional Children, 56*(4), 306–313.

Pogrow, S. (1993). The forgotten question in the Chapter I debate: Why are the students having so much trouble learning? *Education Week, 26,* 36.

Pressley, M. (2000). What should comprehension instruction be the instruction of? In M. L. Kamil, P. B. Mosenthal, P. D. Pearson, & R. Barr (Eds.), *Handbook of Reading Research* (Vol. III, pp. 546-561). Mahwah, NJ: Erlbaum.

Pressley, M., Allington, R., Morrow, L., Baker, K., Wharton-McDonald, R., Block, C.C., et al. (1998). *The nature of effective first-grade literacy instruction.* Report Series 11007. Albany, NY: The National Research Center on English Learning and Achievement.

Rasinski, T. V. (1990). Effects of repeated reading and listening-while-reading on reading fluency. *Journal of Educational Research 83,*(3), 147–150.

Reid, M. (1990). *The Button Box.* New York: Scott Foresman.

Reutzel, D. R., & Hollingsworth, P. M. (1991). Reading time in school: Effect on fourth graders' performance on a criterion-referenced comprehension test. *Journal of Educational Research 84,* (3), 170–176.

Robb, L. (2000). *Teaching reading in middle school.* New York: Scholastic.

Robbins, C., & Ehri, L. C. (1994). Reading storybooks to kindergartners helps them learn new vocabulary words. *Journal of Educational Psychology 86*(1), pp 54–64.

Rosenblatt, L. (1968). *Literature as exploration.* New York: Nobel and Noble.

Rosenshine, B., & Meister, C. C. (1994). Reciprocal teaching: A review of the research. *Review of Educational Research, 64*(4), 479–530.

Samuels, S. J. (1994). Toward a theory of automatic information processing in reading revisited. In R. B. Ruddell, M. R. Ruddell, & H. Singer (Eds.), *Theoretical models and processes of reading,* (3rd edition, pp. 816–837). Newark, DE: International Reading Association.

Samuels, S. J. (2002). Reading fluency: Its development and assessment. In A. E. Fartstup and S. J. Samuels (Eds.), *What research has to say about reading instruction,* (3rd ed., pp. 166–183). Newark, DE: International Reading Association.

Scanlon, D. M., & Vellutino, F. R. (1996). Prerequisite skills, early instruction, and success in first-grade reading: Selected results from a longitudinal study. *Mental Retardation and Developmental Research Reviews, 2,* 54–63.

Scarborough, H. S. (1998). Early identification of children at risk for reading disabilities: Phonological awareness and some other promising predictors. In B. K. Shapiro, P. J. Accardo, & A. J. Capute (Eds.), *Specific reading disability: A view of the spectrum* (pp. 77–121). Timonium, MD: York Press.

Scarborough, H. S. (1989). Prediction of reading disability from familial and individual differences. *Journal of Educational Psychology, 81*(1), 101–108.

Senechal, M. (1997). The differential effect of storybook reading on preschoolers' acquisition of expressive and receptive vocabulary. *Journal of Child Language, 24*(1), 123–138.

Seuss, Dr. (1957). *The cat in the hat.* New York: Random House.

Seuss, Dr. (1976). *Hop on pop.* New York: Random House.

Seuss, Dr. (1996). *There's a Wocket in my pocket.* New York: Random House.

Shaywitz, B. A., Fletcher, J. M., & Shaywitz, S. E. (1995). Defining and classifying learning disabilities and attention-deficit/hyperactivity disorder. *Journal of Child Neurology 10* (Supplement 1), S50–S57.

Shaywitz, S. E., Fletcher, J. M., & Shaywitz, B. A. (1994). Issues in the definition and classification of attention deficit disorder. *Topics in Language Disorders 14*(4),1–25.

Shaywitz, S. E., Shaywitz, B. A., Fletcher, J. M., & Escobar, M. D. (1992). Prevalence of reading disability in boys and girls: Results of the Connecticut Longitudinal Study. *Journal of the American Medical Association, 264,* 998–1002.

Snow, C. E., Burns, S. M. , & Griffin, P. (Eds.) (1998). *Preventing reading difficulties in young children.* Washington, DC: National Academy of Education.

Spilich, G. J., Vesonder, G. T., Chiesi, H. L., and Voss, J. F. (1979). Text processing of domain-related information for individuals with high and low domain knowledge. *Journal of Verbal Learning and Verbal Behavior, 18,* 275-290.

Stahl, S., & Vancil, S. (1986). Discussion is what makes semantic maps work in vocabulary instruction. *Reading Teacher, 40,* 62–69.

Stahl, S. A., Duffy-Hester, A. M., and Stahl, K. A. D. (1998). Everything you wanted to know about phonics (but were afraid to ask). Reading Research Quarterly, 33, 338-355.

Stallings, J. A. (1980a). Effects of instruction base on the Madeline Hunter model on students' achievement: Findings from a follow-through project. *Elementary School Journal 87,* (2), 117–138.

Stallings, J. A. (1980b). Allocated academic learning time revisited, or beyond time on task. *Educational Researcher, 8*(11), 11-16.

Stanovich, K. E. (1986). Matthew effects in reading: Some consequences of individual differences in the acquisition of literacy. *Reading Research Quarterly 21,* 360–407.

Stanovich, K. E. (1993). Romance and reality (Distinguished Educator Series). *The Reading Teacher, 47,* 280–291.

Stanovich, K. E., & Siegel, L. S. (1994). Phenotypic performance profiles of children with reading disabilities: A regression-based test of the phonological-core variable-difference model. *Journal of Educational Psychology, 86,* 24–53.

Stotsky, S. (1983). Research on reading/writing relationships: A synthesis and suggested directions. *Language Arts, 60,* 627–642.

Stringfield, S., & Teddlie, C. (1991). Observers as predictors of schools' multi-year outlier status. *Elementary School Journal, 91*(4), 357–376.

Sulzby, E. (1996). Roles of oral and written language as children approach conventional literacy. In C. Pontecorvo, M. Orsolini, B. Burge, & L. B. Resnick, (Eds.), *Early test construction in children* (pp. 25–46). Hillsdale, NJ: Erlbaum.

Sulzby, E., & Teale, W. H. (1991). Emergent literacy. In R. Barr, M. L. Kamil, P. Mosenthal, & P. D. Pearson (Eds.), *Handbook of reading research* (Vol. 2, pp. 727–757). New York: Longman.

Taylor B. M., Frye, B. J., & Maruyama, G. M. (1990). Time spent reading and reading growth. *American Educational Research Journal 27*(2), 351–362.

Terban, M. (1987). *Mad as a wet hen.* Boston: Clarion.

Tierney, R. J., Readence, J. E. and Dishner, E. K. (1990). *Reading strategies and practices: A compendium* (3rd ed.). Boston: Allyn and Bacon.

Treiman, R., & Zukowski, A. (1991). Children's sensitivity to syllables, onsets, rimes, and phonemes. *Journal of Experimental Child Psychology, 61,* 193–215.

Tracey, D., Brooks, G., Cronin, J., & Woo, D. (1998). *The nature of effective first-grade literacy instruction.* Report Series 11007. Albany, NY: The National Research Center on English Learning and Achievement.

Venezky, R. L. & Winfield, L. F. (1979). Schools that succeed beyond expectations in reading. *In Studies in education. Technical Report No. 1.* Newark: University of Delaware.

Wagner, R. K., Torgeson, J. K., & Roshotte, C. A. (1994). Development of reading-related phonological processing abilities: New evidence of bi-directional causality from a latent variable longitudinal study. *Developmental Psychology 30*(1): 73–87.

Wilson, E.A. (1995). *Reading at the middle and high school levels: Building active readers across the curriculum.* Arlington, VA: Educational Research Service.

Wood, K. (1984). Probable passages: A writing strategy. *The Reading Teacher, 37,* 496-499.

Wylie, R. E. & Durrell, D. D. (1970). Teaching vowels through phonograms. *Elementary English 47*(6), P. 787–91.

Yopp, H. (1988).The validity and reliability of phonemic awareness tests. *Reading Research Quarterly, 23,* 159–177.

❧ Index ❧

✴ About the Author ✦

Karen Tankersley is currently in her fifth year as Associate Superintendent for Educational Services in a rapidly growing school district in Surprise, Arizona in the Phoenix metropolitan area. Originally, a linguist with a Bachelor of Liberal Arts degree in French and a minor in German and English, she has an extensive background in language and language acquisition issues. Tankersley also holds a Master of Arts in Reading and a Doctor of Philosophy degree in Educational Leadership and Policy Studies from Arizona State University. In her early career, Tankersley spent 10 years as a foreign language teacher, reading specialist, and teacher of the gifted and talented. She also served for 12 years as a principal in schools recognized for their outstanding achievement and performance. She has taught at the university level and serves as a consultant to schools and districts around the nation on literacy and school improvement issues. She has published articles in several educational journals including *Educational Leadership*. Tankersley can be reached by e-mail at her Web site, www.threadsofreading.com.

At the time of publication, the following ASCD resources were available; for the most up-to-date information about ASCD resources, go to www.ascd.org. ASCD stock numbers are noted in parentheses.

Networks

Visit the ASCD Web site (www.ascd.org) and search for "networks" for information about professional educators who have formed groups around topics such as "Language, Literacy and Literature: Whole Language Perspective and Practice." Look in the "Network Directory" for current facilitators' addresses and phone numbers.

Print Products

Capturing All of the Reader Through the Reading Assessment System: Practical Applications for Guiding Strategic Readers by Rachel Billmeyer (#303358)

Literacy Leadership for Grades 5–12 by Rosemary Taylor and Valerie Doyle Collins (#103022)

The Multiple Intelligences of Reading and Writing: Making the Words Come Alive by Thomas Armstrong (#102280)

Reading Strategies for the Content Areas: An ASCD Action Tool by Sue Beers and Lou Howell (#703109)

Teaching Beginning Reading and Writing with the Picture Word Inductive Model by Emily F. Calhoun

Teaching Reading in the Content Areas: If Not Me, Then Who? (2nd ed.) by Rachel Billmeyer and Mary Lee Barton

Videotapes

The Brain and Reading Video Series (3 videos) (#499207)

How to Use Prewriting Strategies (#403115)

Implementing a Reading Program in Secondary Schools (tape and facilitator's guide) (#402033)

Reading in the Content Areas Video Series (3-tape series and online facilitator's guide) (#402029)

For more information, visit us on the World Wide Web (http://www.ascd.org), send an e-mail message to member@ascd.org, call the ASCD Service Center (1-800-933-ASCD or 703-578-9600, then press 2), send a fax to 703-575-5400, or write to Information Services, ASCD, 1703 N. Beauregard St., Alexandria, VA 22311-1714 USA.